Acknowledgements

This book would not have gotten past the rough draft stage without the help of a number of friends and family members.

I want to thank Michelle Ziemba for her work in proofing, editing, and making some good suggestions for this book. I may have finished this work without her help, but it would never have come out so well. I take full responsibility for any typographical or grammatical errors in this book. I admit to rewriting and adding substantial material after the edits were completed.

I also want to thank my family: my husband, for allowing me to talk candidly about his condition and our marriage; and our sons for putting up with us. It's hard enough to have a father with bipolar disorder, but to also have a mother who is writing a book about it in her spare time (what's that?) has to be pretty stressful.

I want to thank my son Troy Jr. for drawing the cover artwork.

I want to thank the members of my support groups who sent me ideas and encouraged me to finish this book and who kept me sane all the way through.

I want to thank you—for reading this book.

Contents

Introduction

Welcome to **Love Has Its Ups And Downs**. *I'm sorry you belong here, but happy that you found me.*

There will be people who tell you that life with a husband or wife who has bipolar disorder is simply impossible—and they could be right. Sometimes it really is impossible. If you can accept that this will not be the life you signed up for and that this disorder could become so destructive that you will be called upon to start your life over at some time—you take a lot of the pressure off and you just might be one whose marriage survives.

Maybe you've been wearing some rose-colored glasses, believing that if you ignore the disorder it will go away. That isn't going to happen. Bipolar disorder is a progressive illness that will continue to get worse unless it is treated.

It is also a cycling illness that can trick you when your spouse cycles through a period of relatively normal stability. You may think you've got this thing under control, but the cycle continues and pretty soon you are in the middle of an episode, wondering what happened and how you are ever going to survive.

I don't know where you are in this process, but I can assume you've got some questions or you wouldn't bother to read this. I can also assume that you really want to make this marriage work or you would just file for divorce and get over it.

I've been where you are now. We went through the years of unexplained mood swings and chaos before the diagnosis, then all of the trial and error in treating the illness after that. I am not living happily ever after—that only happens in fairy tales. I have a very normal real marriage with all the normal problems. And I have a husband who has a serious mental illness to top it all off. But we are making it work, and I am happy to share with you just how we are doing it to give you some ideas how you can do the same.

There are some important things you need to know if you want to have a good life under these trying circumstances. I've learned these lessons from over 20 years of living with a bipolar husband—many of those years he was undiagnosed and untreated.

I've learned from online support groups where some really wonderful people have shared their lives and ideas. Search for BPSO (Bipolar Significant Other) on the Internet for an email support group. I am part of a Christian online support group at <u>BipolarPrayer@yahoogroups.com</u>. You are welcome to join us.

I've learned from books, some of which are mentioned at the end of the appropriate chapter. But mostly I've learned by trial and error. Follow my lead, but skip my mistakes. It's a long bumpy ride on the "bipolar roller coaster," but we'll survive.

That's what this book is about. If that's what you are looking for, welcome to the club nobody wants to belong to. You're in good company.

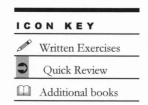

ICON KEY

✎ Written Exercises

⮡ Quick Review

📖 Additional books

Put On Your Own Oxygen Mask First

If you've ever traveled by plane, you've heard the instruction; "If the oxygen masks come down, please put your own mask on first, then you can safely help others." You can't help anyone if you stop breathing, right? It makes perfect sense.

You know it; I know it; everyone knows it; but doing it can be a problem. We always think, "Well, I'll be fine," and we don't even notice that we might be ready to pass out from the lack of oxygen because we are so busy trying to put a mask on someone who is fighting every step of the way.

You need every ounce of strength you have to support someone with bipolar disorder. Allowing your strength to be diminished by not taking care of your own needs may turn out to be the thing that causes you all to go under together.

The first half of this book will tell you what you need to do to protect your own safety, sanity, and health. If you think this section should come second, you have a lot to learn. There are lots of books out there that tell you how to take care of someone with a serious mental illness, but most of them seem to assume that you can just drop everything and wrap your whole life up in caring for someone who may not even welcome your help. Following that advice may be good for your spouse in the short term, but if you use up all of your energy on the disorder and don't have any left for yourself or your marriage, it won't last.

Put On Your Own Oxygen Mask First! You can't save anyone else until you save yourself. You are worth saving.

I will tell you how to stay physically strong and healthy. I will tell you how to stay emotionally healthy. I will tell you how to avoid being dragged under by the insanity that inevitably enters into this life. Maybe you will find other ways to solve your problems—and I'd be thrilled to hear what they are. Maybe you will use some of what I have to offer. I pray that it works as well for you as it has for me.

Maybe you will find that you have to end the marriage to save your sanity. It is not a failure if you can't maintain the marriage. This is not an easy situation, and the odds are against you. But maybe you will be able to make your marriage work. Maybe you will find treatments that work. Maybe you will beat the odds. I hope that you can.

If you just use the ideas in this book to survive and escape with your own sanity intact, we will still be successful. Not every person with bipolar is marriage material and there's nothing you or I can do about it. We didn't cause this disorder. We can't control another person's behavior. We can't cure an incurable illness. We are not gods, and we need to face that fact right now and get it out of the way.

Boundaries

You can't control other people so you must control yourself.

What are boundaries? Why do I need to set boundaries? What can boundaries do for me? Where do I start setting my own boundaries, and how do I know whether my boundaries are working for me?

Boundaries are the lines we draw around ourselves to protect us. They are like a privacy fence that keeps out intruders. Boundaries are not intended to control other people. They are drawn to show where our interests end and how close others can get before we feel threatened and react.

You might think that setting up boundaries means that the marriage isn't very healthy, that there's some sort of power play going on, but this couldn't be further from the truth. All healthy relationships have strong boundaries in place. It's just that with healthy partners, many of the boundaries are known but unspoken. You don't have to tell a healthy spouse not to spend the rent money on some neat gadget or not to run around the house screaming and throwing things. Healthy adults know what is likely to happen if they have an affair. You don't have to tell them.

There's really no trick to setting boundaries, and there's no right or wrong either. There's just what works for you and what doesn't. It may take some work to define your own boundaries if you haven't done this before. You keep trying until something works. You may have to think through boundaries that are normally taken for granted, but think them through and make plans that are specific to your experience.

When you start setting boundaries, it might help to think of the things that hurt you the most or that you worry about the most. What thing sends you running for cover? Think of boundaries as the window screen that keeps the mosquitoes from flying into your bedroom. What are the "mosquitoes" that sneak into your life? Is it violence or threats of violence? Is it a refusal to accept treatment that keeps your partner from being stable enough to be helpful? Is it the instability itself? Is it not being sure when you're hearing the truth? Is it infidelity of some sort?

Whatever that thing is, that's your mosquito in the bedroom. Write it down on a piece of paper or type it into a note file or record it on a tape recorder—it just makes things more real and concrete if we can see it. Don't just think it, write it down. (There is a form for this purpose at the end of this chapter.) Those are your boundaries.

OK, what would keep that mosquito out of the bedroom? It would be great if the mosquito could just decide that it doesn't want to go there, but you can't control the mosquito—you can only control yourself.

What can you do? Can you take the kids and go for a walk or a drive or a visit when certain things happen? Can you separate yourself physically—another room, a friend's house, your own apartment, whatever it takes, for as long as it takes for the "mosquito" to go away? Write down what you can do. Make a list of possibilities; throw in anything that comes to mind—some of the most farfetched ideas can turn into workable plans when you have time to think about it.

When you do have some free time—ok, take the list to the bathroom if you have to and concentrate on it while you take your shower or bath—decide on a specific plan of action for each scenario. This is your plan to protect your boundaries. Write it out or tell a friend or do something to make it real to you.

You can tell people your boundaries so that they know your expectations and can make decisions about their own behavior. For example, "If you raise your voice to me or speak to me in that tone, I'm not going to continue the conversation and I'm going to leave the room until you calm down."

In the case of serious mental illness, you may also need a few ideas that are "for emergency use only"—like calling the police and get a restraining order the next time you are abused. If you think knowing the boundary might change behavior, announce it. But don't dare announce it before you are prepared to follow through—not even once. It doesn't take long to get a reputation as someone who doesn't follow through and you don't want that reputation.

Boundaries work with everyone in your life. You can send the kids to their rooms when they are upsetting you (beats the alternative of beating them or screaming at them when you come to the end of your rope) or tell your boss or teacher that you will report disrespectful behavior and then follow through.

That's setting boundaries. It's being assertive, not aggressive. It's putting your own oxygen mask on first so you have a chance to rescue someone else. It's survival.

One example of a boundary for living with a person with bipolar disorder that has come up in support groups is "I will not live with an untreated person with bipolar disorder." Some people find this boundary hard to maintain, while others hold firmly to it. This boundary comes into play when your spouse decides that "I'm not sick, I don't need medication" and you have to ask them to pick up any personal property and find other housing, not because you are angry or because you don't love them, but because you "will not live with a person with untreated bipolar disorder."

Boundaries can keep things simple and unemotional. You can state them as facts and follow through on them very matter-of-factly. "I will continue this conversation with you when we can talk calmly" is another way of saying "I will not listen to ranting and raving when you are manic." This boundary turns into "if you continue to speak to me that way, I will leave until we both calm down and that might be a very long time." You can repeat the boundary word for word—and not leave room for discussion.

Boundaries are very personal. I might not be terribly upset by ranting and raving or by coming home to someone who hasn't been out of bed all day, but I might be bothered by someone withdrawing money from my bank account and not leaving enough to pay the power bill. My husband knows that if he messes up the bank account, he is responsible for fixing it and I am free to go visit friends or sit in the library until he gets the lights or the water or whatever back on. He knows that if I have to sleep with no power, I won't be in a very good mood. You might have other boundaries.

The point of a boundary is to protect YOU. If it doesn't make you feel safe, it isn't protecting you.

Sometimes boundaries are put up to protect other people. You, as a stable adult, are responsible to protect any children that are living in your home, so you will have to establish boundaries on their behalf—while it is true that we all have our own boundaries, it is also true that children, especially in a parent-child relationship, are not usually able to create and maintain their own boundaries.

Don't wait until your child comes to you or until you see signs of depression or fear. Look at things from a child's point of view and create the boundaries that you would want if you were a child. It is better to be a little overprotective at this point, I think. Children are very vulnerable to abuse from a parent or step-parent, so give them big boundaries. Our youngest son knew enough to go to his older brother's apartment when his father was in episode. It gave him space to be safe. Is there a chance that your child will be home alone with a raving maniac? What can YOU do to avoid that? What can the child do? Setting up a safe-house with a neighbor or family member will make everyone feel more secure.

It may be uncomfortable for you to take on the whole job of disciplining your children, but if your spouse gets carried away with this task or it is too emotionally charged you have to do it yourself. Make it a boundary and maintain it like a life depends on it—it may.

A boundary can ONLY protect you and your children. It cannot infringe on another person's safety or security. A boundary can't force people to do what you want. It puts all of the choices in their hands and lets them know more accurately what those choices are. For example, if a person becomes violent when manic, there might be a choice of taking appropriate medications and following therapy instructions, going peacefully to the hospital when early signs of mania are noticed or moving out so that the family is safe.

A person with hypersexual tendencies might have to choose between ending all affairs and submitting to lab tests for STDs or leaving the family home.

It might be a choice between talking calmly and talking to the wall because everyone will leave when the ranting and raving commences.

Boundaries are NOT ultimatums, they are options.

Boundaries should be established when you are calm and relaxed, though they may need to be changed or new ones added when things happen that you didn't plan for. It works best if you have some general rules that you can adapt to a variety of situations. Just having a place to go when you feel threatened for any reason may come in handy—and it's not entirely a coincidence that when you have a safe place to go, you don't feel the need to escape as often.

Practice using boundaries with all of the people you come into contact with. Boundaries keep you safe from all kinds of people in all kinds of situations. If you have boundaries with friends, co-workers, and other family members, you won't be singling anyone out—it isn't personal, it's just a tool that you use to keep your life safe.

You will avoid a lot of unnecessary frustration when you give up trying to control other people and concentrate on controlling the person you actually have power over—yourself.

Boundaries or Codependent Behavior

Sometimes when you enforce boundaries, you will end up taking on additional responsibilities for yourself and this might be interpreted as enabling or codependent. It is nearly impossible for most people outside the relationship to see the difference, so you may even be accused of this by others.

People who have issues with codependence have an unhealthy need to keep the other person weak and needy—it makes them feel powerful. They will continue to fix things for their partner even when the natural consequences would force the person into improving their behavior—for example, keeping them out of jail or the hospital when it is warranted, paying drinking or gambling debts so that the person can return to drinking or gambling or overspending on other things.

People who have a mentally ill spouse would often give anything to be able to share the power and responsibility, but they have learned that they cannot always do this. They have a very normal need to keep enough money in the bank to have the bills paid. They have a very normal need to know that they aren't sleeping with someone who has picked up some life-threatening disease through promiscuous behavior.

There is nothing wrong, unhealthy, codependent or enabling about cleaning up the messes that affect you or your family, even if you didn't make them. Some of the things you do would be wrong if your spouse were capable of doing them or of learning from the mistakes—but with mental illness, that isn't usually the case.

Boundaries Put Into Practice

Use these charts to write your own boundaries. Make sure that each situation is clear, the reaction is not punitive, but will serve to protect your health, safety and sanity. Don't discuss boundaries that you aren't prepared to defend or you will not be expected to defend any of your boundaries.

Boundary Defense Worksheet

(Use a separate copy for each boundary)

Boundary:	
	Possible ways to defend boundary:
1	
2	
3	
4	
5	
6	
7	
8	

MY BOUNDARIES

Boundary: I need ...	Consequence: I will...
To avoid a person exhibiting dangerous symptoms of mental illness.	Be part of the treatment team so I know what medications are prescribed and I will leave or ask you to leave if medications are not being taken.
To both talk calmly when we disagree	Leave the area and refuse to continue the discussion until we are both calm.

Review

Boundaries are factual statements about what you need to feel comfortable. They are not used to control other people. They are used to present options to another person so that they will know what to expect when they engage in behaviors that harm or threaten you. They are used to plan for yourself what you will do when others engage in behaviors that harm or threaten you.

Books about Boundaries:

Boundaries in Marriage or *Boundaries* by Henry Cloud and John Townsend

Your Health

Although bipolar disorder is not contagious, it can sure make you sick.

It's unavoidable to get worn down from time to time, but you have to care for yourself if you intend to care for anyone else. Do you really want to end up in the hospital with a mystery virus while your bipolar spouse is left to deal with everything? (Don't even let your imagination run with that thought.) I didn't think so. You have to do everything you can to stay healthy.

Almost everyone who deals with a bipolar spouse for many years will eventually develop health issues. The mood swings take a toll. Waiting for the next episode keeps you on edge. Walking on eggshells on those days when breathing seems to set off a violent reaction is hard work.

The stress level for a spouse is probably the greatest because unlike the parent of a bipolar child, you do have the option of filing for divorce, there will be friends and family members who will see you suffering and believe that you are bringing it on yourself by not divorcing. But don't assume you will get support if you leave because others will demonize you for walking out on a sick person. This Catch 22 may be the ultimate stressor.

At one time medical people believed that all disease was caused by germs, viruses and chemicals. Although that is true, we have learned that the human body is capable of fighting off just about everything that attacks it when there aren't too many attacks at the same time. But even if there don't appear to be a lot of attacks going on, the daily stress level can have a major impact on your immune system.

While stress is distracting your immune system, all sorts of nasty things can sneak into your body. And because you may have to do more than your share to support and care for your family with significantly less help than you'd get from a healthy mate, you may tend to allow yourself to get physically and emotionally worn down. If you have those two strikes against you (stress and exhaustion) every little virus or bacterium that you run into has the upper hand. Unless you consciously work on keeping yourself healthy, you don't have a chance.

You can't really eliminate all of the stress in your life and trying to do so would cause more stress. There are things you can do to make your stress less wearing on your body—we'll talk a bit more about the stress specific to living with a bipolar spouse in the chapter on detaching.

There are other things, important things that you can do for yourself to build your immunity and strength.

Sleep

Most adults need close to eight hours of sleep every night at approximately the same time every night. If you are living on less than six or more than 10 hours of sleep, you may want to discuss this with your doctor—it could perfectly normal for you, but it could be a problem that you need help with.

Sleep may not be an issue for you if you are waking up refreshed and renewed and ready to start the day. But if you are waking up feeling like you just want to roll over and go back to sleep or if you are groggy after getting up, you may want to work on your sleep habits.

Start by counting back eight hours, or more if you are still not feeling rested, from the time that you have to get up. Have an established bedtime for yourself and work toward being in bed at that time every night and within two hours of that time even on week-ends and holidays.

About an hour or two before bedtime—perhaps after you tuck in any young children—start a bedtime routine that includes relaxing tasks like taking a warm shower or bath, turning out or dimming the lights and having a light snack, then reading, playing solitaire, or doing some other activity that is not overly stimulating.

Listening to soft music or watching something mindless on TV works for some people. If the evening news just upsets you, watch the early news and skip it at night. Some people find the flickering lights of the TV to be too stimulating. Video games are generally a poor choice—there is an addicting quality so that if you start a game, you won't quit when you get sleepy.

When bedtime comes, get into bed, turn out the lights and close your eyes. It may not work every time, but it will work eventually for most people. Don't watch the clock—but if you feel like it's been a long time, check. If you don't fall asleep in ten or twenty minutes, get up and do something. Have a light snack, read, get a drink of water, wash your face and hands, whatever you find calming.

If you find that you still can't get to sleep, that you can't stay asleep or that you don't feel rested when you wake up, talk to a doctor. There may be something more going on or you may need medication to help with sleep until you can get into a sleep routine. Sleeping pills are no substitute for a bedtime routine and will stop working with continued use, so use them as a last resort and work on other tactics.

Eat

When stressed out, two common eating problems may occur: either you grab a carton of Hagen Das and a box of Chips Ahoy or you stop eating altogether. Both of these possibilities are unhealthy and both of these possibilities can stress you out more if they continue.

Eating high sugar or high fat food is comforting for the moment, but the rush wears off and leaves you feeling drained. Other types of food are better for regular snacks. Keeping raw fruits and vegetables in the house, ready to eat in the fridge or in a fruit bowl, makes it easier to grab a healthy snack. This is also great for your bipolar partner, as junk food does seem to increase symptoms in some people with bipolar disorder.

Plan a regular menu for yourself and your family. Use the USDA food pyramid or ask a nutritionist for specific help if you have special needs. Include snacks in the menu and avoid fad diets and fast foods.

Look into one of the "Once a Month Cooking" or "Freezer Cooking" plans if you don't have time to cook every day. You don't need to follow the menu plan or the recipes in the book, but do consider the idea of precooking some meals in advance and leaving them in the freezer for emergencies. I just do a few things—chopping more onions and green peppers than I need and freezing the rest for another meal, browning half of the large package of ground beef and packing meal sized portions in the freezer precooked and making and freezing hamburger patties with what's left. Find ideas that work for you and leave the rest.

If "real meals" seem too expensive, try cutting back on meats and stick to foods that are "in season" and plentiful. Most people will find that eating a balanced diet is cheaper than fast foods, processed snack foods or any of the typical junk food diets. You can't eat steak and potatoes every night, but you can eat healthy.

Plan grocery shopping trips to pick up several days worth of groceries and have food in the house so that you won't be tempted to pick up another frozen pizza, or stop for fast food.

Snack on raw fruit and vegetables or crackers with meat or cheese. They are quick, easy and healthier than candy and chips. Celery and peanut butter is a healthy snack. Yes, there is fat in peanut butter, but compared to most other protein foods, it's not enough to worry about.

Drink

This should probably fit in with the eating part, but it is so important and so overlooked that I gave it a heading to make it stand out. It is important that you keep your body hydrated, that you get enough water. Most people are aware of this, and some are keeping a bottle of water to drink through the day.

As important as it is that you drink something, it is also important to drink the right things. Some drinks can actually dry your body out—many soft drinks, coffee, alcohol and even a few poorly designed energy drinks. Try to drink a glass of water at least five times a day. It won't hurt to flavor the water with lemon or drink mix or to substitute fruit juice for two or three of the servings, but don't substitute anything with caffeine or carbonation.

You may be in the early stages of dehydration and not feel thirsty, but dehydration is one stress that is easy (and cheap) to avoid. That burned out feeling that you get in the middle of the day may be thirst more than anything else. When in doubt, grab a glass of water. It won't hurt.

Exercise

Regular exercise does not have to be an hour at the gym every evening. It can be done with your regular work or it can be something that helps you relax. Take the stairs instead of the elevator. Walk or ride a bicycle to work or to do errands. Hang the laundry on a clothes line instead of throwing it in the dryer. Or swim laps on a hot day.

You don't have to do much, just a little more than you are doing now. In a few weeks, increase your activity a bit more. Slow, steady progress is more healthy and safe than trying to go from couch potato to marathon runner in a few weeks. Yes, your bipolar spouse may try going from watching sports on TV to being an athlete, but we call that ramping up—not getting healthy.

If you are not happy with your weight or physical condition, appropriate exercise is the most important thing you can do to fix that. It's not a quick, easy fix. It's a healthy, reliable method. Take your time and do it right. Trying to do too much too soon may cause physical damage or may just be too much work or pain for you to want to keep at it long enough to make a difference.

Check-ups

Don't wait until you are sick to see a doctor. Most healthy adults rarely visit a doctor for a check-up, but because you are a care-giver, count that as a risk factor and make a regular annual pilgrimage. You can avoid a lot of major stuff by catching it while it's minor. Get your cholesterol down BEFORE the heart attack. Get the blood pressure under control BEFORE the stroke. You don't have time to sit in a hospital, so take care of your health while you are still healthy enough to do it.

Don't expect the doctor to find everything in a standard physical. Tell the doctor that you have been under significant stress, describe any symptoms or problems that you have noticed no matter how minor, and have any tests that are requested completed in a timely manner. Use any experience you've had working with the psychiatrist to gather your confidence to work with your own doctor. Ask questions and get answers.

If a problem is found, study your options and start treatment as soon as possible. If there are decisions to be made, ask as many questions as it takes and read everything you can get your hands on, and then make the decision. Most medical problems only get worse if you hesitate to treat them.

Health Care Plans

Write out your own health care plan on the following charts. Make a plan and work the plan to make your body work for you

First, get a physical so you know if you need to make any special adjustments. Use each chart for two or three until it becomes a habit for you. Feel free to make copies of the charts or to create your own charts. If you create a chart that you find really helpful, send me a copy to share in the next edition of this book.

Write the date of your last physical and any special findings. If it has been more than one year make an appointment now and write the date of your next physical.

Date of physical	Findings/Advice

Write out your bedtime plan here. The idea is not to have a strict schedule to follow, but to have some sort of plan to get to bed at a reasonable hour. Start watching the clock in the evening with an eye to wrapping things up before you need to start your bedtime routine.

Bedtime Plan

Time:	Activity:
	Lie down and close eyes

Sample Meal Plan

Use a chart for each day. I filled in this sample.

Daily	Breakfast	Snack	Lunch	Snack	Dinner	Snack
2-4 Fruit	Orange Juice	Grapes			Peach	
3-5 Veggies			Peas and Carrots		Potato salad	Carrots
6-11 Cereals	Cereal	Bread	Pasta	Crackers	Rolls	Crackers
2-3 Dairy	Milk	Yogurt		Cheese		
2-3 Protein			Fish (tuna)		Hamburger	

Balanced Daily Menu Plan

Fill in what you will eat for each meal under the appropriate food group.

daily	Breakfast	Snack	Lunch	Snack	Dinner	Snack
2-4 Fruit						
3-5 Veggies						
6-11 Cereals						
2-3 Dairy						
2-3 Protein						

Make a check for each glass of water you drink--5 a day for 7 days.

	1	2	3	4	5
Sunday					
Monday					
Tuesday					
Wednesday					
Thursday					
Friday					
Saturday					

Review

If you want to help anyone else, you have to stay healthy yourself. There is a reason "diet, exercise and rest" is the cliché answer to so many health problems: it works. You can't change your life in a day, but you can start today. One step at a time, you can change your life.

Cooking Books:

Frozen Assets: How to Cook for a Day and Eat for a Month, by Deborah Taylor-Hough. The original "once a month" cookbooks seemed a bit fancy for my family. This one is much more practical and we like the recipes.

Do It (for) Yourself

You deserve a break--today.

Maybe nobody has mentioned this to you, but
every human alive deserves a little fun every day. You may have even
received the advice from a doctor or therapist—to do something nice for
yourself once in a while. What you choose to do will depend on what you
enjoy, but it is a very good idea to find something that you enjoy.

If you have trouble doing something nice for yourself because you
feel like you don't have the time, don't have the money, or don't even
know where to start—STOP! You are looking for fun in all the
wrong places. You don't need to steal resources from the family in
order to treat yourself to a bit of happiness. Having done parenting,
poverty, and general insanity I feel somewhat qualified to offer a list
of ideas to get you started in finding ways to put on your own oxygen
mask first—how to give to yourself so that you have something left
to give to others.

1.) Nature therapy: go out into a yard or park and actually look at
the flowers and the birds and the small animals—it may help
you to focus if you have a camera or if you take a sketch pad,
but those things are purely optional. A walk in the woods is
calming if you have a wooded area nearby. A walk on the
beach is nice too, if there aren't a lot of people there.

2.) Create a nature sanctuary: a bird feeder or bird house to
attract the type of bird that makes you smile could be a very
worthwhile investment. You can always make one yourself or
find one at a thrift store or yard sale.

3.) You can plant a garden and grow things to eat with your
family. Or just grow pretty flowers.

4.) Art/Craft therapy: grab the camera, the sketch pad, scraps of
materials, a notebook, yarn or whatever you enjoy working

with. Start small or make something that you'd buy otherwise if money is an issue.

5.) Performance art therapy: Sing, dance, play an instrument. Whether it's karaoke night or guitar lessons or just singing loudly in the shower, perform with all of your might.

6.) Bake: cookies, bread, cakes, or crème brulee. Get creative in the kitchen. I hate having to cook a family dinner every night, but I have fun doing special things. I've even invested in some specialized equipment for the kitchen.

7.) Read: The library is a nice source of free books, and there are thrift shops and yard sales where you can grow your own library with pocket change. I used to find books during the library story time—while the little ones were busy listening to stories.

8.) Borrow the tools and materials for your next project, don't buy them. Check out http://Neighborrow.com and share books, small appliances and tools with other people in your area. Just looking at the list of things you can borrow in your neighborrowhood might inspire you to try something new.

9.) Go to SecondLife.com and create a whole new life for yourself. You can even create a new YOU. Travel the world at the click of a mouse button and meet interesting people or see the sights on your own.

10.) If you enjoy a nice long hot bath, try adding some nice bubble bath and a few candles around the tub, then lotion and powder for afterwards. Watch for sales on bath and spa items and create an oasis in your bathroom. Watch for after-Christmas sales for supplies. You can find nice sets to do your own manicure and pedicure—much less expensive than paying to have it done.

11.) Pet therapy: if you have a pet in the house, take some time to talk to the animals—petting or brushing a cat or dog is very relaxing (unless you let things get out of hand or you take a long haired dog for a walk in the woods) and even a goldfish will listen politely to all of your problems, never argue with you, and keep your secrets.

12.)Devotions: even if you do a devotional with the family, try getting up a few minutes early or carving a few minutes of time somewhere else and spending the time in prayer and Bible reading. You can get calendars or join an email list to get a verse or two every day.

13.)Write pages: I started doing this when I read The Artist Way. Write three pages every morning of stream of consciousness stuff. This gets all those mangled thoughts and worries out of your head and onto paper so you can deal with them or forget them. I don't think there is any magic in the three pages that she assigns, but it is long enough that you have to write something more than: "Here I am writing my stupid pages again. I can't think of a thing to say. Why did I ever decide to start doing this?"

14.)Develop any passion that you might have. You don't have to make a career out of it, but don't rule it out. Just take one small step toward your impossible dreams and remember that nothing is impossible. Take one class at the local community college, read a book and actually follow the advice, talk to others who share your passion. Tomorrow you can take another step.

15.)Call or visit an old friend. I just found my best friend from grade school online and have been getting reacquainted. It's easy to lose track of people we care about when we get overwhelmed with our own life. Take a few minutes and look up that old friend and have a nice chat. Or make a new friend—call someone interesting from church or work or the neighborhood.

16.)Listen to music that makes you feel good while you work around the house. Most of the radios in the house are set to my husband's favorite type of music, but I know where my stations are and I also have some recorded music.

17.)Hang the laundry on a clothesline. I call it my solar-wind powered clothes drier. Nobody bothers you while you hang laundry because they are afraid you'll get them to help. It's quiet and outside and it saves on the energy bills. Nothing like a little fresh air and exercise to make you feel alive. My mother always liked mowing the lawn—nobody bothers you when you are mowing the lawn.

18.) Take a nap in the afternoon.

19.) Make a list of things that YOU like to do and find ways of doing them like I am doing with this list. I'm sure there are things that would make you happy that wouldn't work for me or that I just haven't thought to include. Make a list of ideas and keep it handy.

20.) Do nothing. My last vacation was spent at home doing nothing. I've never enjoyed a vacation more. I watched birds, splashed in the backyard pool, read books under a tree, and ate salads and sandwiches and things my husband cooked on the grill—on paper plates.

What you do to put a little fun back into your life could be anything that you can imagine. While I don't necessarily believe that everyone can be successful at anything they set out to do—I KNOW that no one has ever been successful at anything until after they set out to do it. I also know that you don't need to be a great artist to enjoy the creative process, and even if you sing off key, you can still make a joyful noise. When you take fun too seriously it stops being fun.

My Own Do It For Myself List:

Make a list of the things you would like to do that are fun for you. They don't have to be big exciting things—but they can be. They don't have to be things you can do any time without planning—but some of them should be. What can you do for YOU?

Idea	Tried

Add one of these ideas to your "TO DO" list at least once a week, daily if possible. Do not select just one and do the same thing over and over. It is fine to repeat, but get some variety in there, too.

My Bucket List

Maybe you've seen the movie, or maybe you've just heard the expression, but most people have a few ideas about things that they would like to do before they "kick the bucket." Maybe you've always wanted to see a Broadway Play, or the Grand Canyon, or the Eiffel Tower. Maybe you want to go scuba diving or sky diving. Make the list concrete by writing it down, and then start working on a plan to make some of those goals a reality.

Item	Need to do first	Time needed	Time started

Detach

*You didn't cause it, you can't control it,
and you can't cure it.*

There is a famous prayer that says "God grant me the serenity to accept
the things I cannot change, the courage to change the things I can, and
the wisdom to know the difference." It's a good prayer for someone who
is dealing with any sort of mental illness because it is tempting to believe
that if we love someone enough, if we pray long and hard enough, if we
do everything the doctors tell us, that somehow we can change a mentally
ill person, that we can fix what's broken and go on with a normal life.

Your first step in dealing with having a bipolar spouse is accepting that
you can change yourself any time, but you can't change another person.
All change must come from inside that person. The sooner you stop
banging your head against THAT wall, the sooner you will be able to go
on with your life and as one of the women who runs an online support
group says "have a great life anyway," which she tells me came from
Amy Catherine White   (NAMI-NYC Metro Teen Support Group
leader).

Detaching is refusing to let things bother you when you can't do anything
about them. If you are spending too much time in irrational arguments,
you can save yourself by learning to detach and stay detached. It may
look like you are giving in, but if it is only words—if there will be time to
come to a real understanding before any action—it's only words.

Detach, detach, detach. If you aren't an expert at this already, now is the
time to work on this skill. It's the only thing I can think of that can get
you through manic and hypo-manic episodes with your own sanity intact.

To detach means to not take things personally, to remember the source
and to let it go without even taking time to think about it. My husband

---

can say some pretty nasty things when he is in episode. I learned to detach out of pure necessity.

At first I'd get fixated on some of his comments—I'd believe them and try to figure out how to be a better person. If only I were a better wife…if only I were a better housekeeper…if only I could fix myself, then everything would be perfect. Eventually, I realized that most of the comments simply weren't true or that they were only true because I was reacting to a difficult situation.

For example, I have never been a great housekeeper—the place here is still cluttered and I'm always behind on the laundry and dishes. But it's not the crime of the century when he kicks his jeans off under the bed and they don't get washed that night.

I know I can't convince him of that when he's in episode, but I can rationalize it myself when I'm thinking clearly. That's a simple way to start detaching from the cruel comments. Look at some you've heard in the past and prove to yourself that they really aren't true, that they are blown way out of proportion, and that although you are not perfect you are not any worse than the other guy. Trust me, you aren't.

I am much easier to get along with if I don't listen to my husband when he gets critical, and he can be really sneaky about it so I have to be careful. Usually if I am feeling crushed and don't know why, when I think it through I realize that he's not even talking about me, he's talking about his own insecurities and fears.

Keeping that firmly in your mind—"he's not really talking about me (even if he believes he is) he is talking about his own insecurities and fears"—can help you to relax and stress less. I've made this an art form and frequently turn my anger into compassion. You can do that, too. It's a survival thing in my world.

If it feels like you can't do anything right, remember that there are a lot of ways of doing things and what works for one person may not work for another. You are not wrong, and no one has the right to impose that idea on you, but you can choose how you will deal with it.

If we get into a disagreement and it's something I feel strongly about, I usually say something like "thank you, but I can handle this myself" and hope he will back off. Sometimes I will give a noncommittal response— "we'll have to look into that more." He's done tons of research on big-screen TVs and motor boats and someday we might even buy one—we might. (We might win the lottery if we play, too.)

If it's something insignificant, I try to go along with what he wants because it gives him a sense of being helpful and part of things. Sometimes he's right and I can always go back to my own ways when he is stable. I don't feel trampled or "put out" because I know that it's my choice.

That's important. You **choose** to go along instead of being forced. You'd be astonished how different it feels. If you give in on insignificant issues or issues where you don't know the best choice yourself, you are more likely to prevail on issues that you consider important and you are more likely to stand your ground if you realize that you are sharing the power.

Ask stable friends or family members to give you a **reality check** from time to time—give them a brief explanation of what's going on, or if they were there at the time, give your own perspective on it and ask "is that how it really was?" or "does that seem right to you?"

I find it easier to deal with the irrational when I can get someone else to verify that it's irrational. Otherwise, I am likely to participate in a marathon argument that gets me nowhere. I might even start to believe that I AM the crazy one. That would be a mistake.

There is no sense arguing for the last word. If you know that you are right but that you aren't going to change a broken mind, you can hold off the fight until such time as you have a rational partner.

If that time never comes, be satisfied to know that you are alright and that you avoided a senseless argument. Getting the last word in one of these arguments is worthless anyway and it is almost always impossible.

Review

To detach, remember that words spoken during an episode may not bear any resemblance to the truth. Becoming emotionally involved with any statement could be hazardous to your health.

Detachment Plan

Write out some of the things you hear that hurt you. Are they true? Write the truth as you know it. If you are tempted to believe what you hear, get a reality check, a second opinion, from someone rational whom you trust.

What I Hear	What I Know
Example: You are selfish!	I do have some needs and wants, but I am more than willing to take turns or share.

Your Family and Friends

Chapter 5

*You've got kids, parents and other people in
your life. Not all of these people need your constant help—and some
can help you.*

It may seem that other people only serve to complicate things—your parents, who think that you could have done better by marrying someone healthy; your spouse's parents, who think you caused their child's problems or at least aren't helping matters; and your children, who love both of their parents but are suffering under the chaos in the house. What's a person to do?

You need to get your family involved if possible or out of the way if necessary, so that they don't feel any more powerless than they are and can understand a bit of what you are dealing with. This will involve doing a bit of research—more work for you—but it will save effort in the long run.

You need to find information or formulate explanations that are at a level that family members can relate. For small children, Eeyore and Tigger can be used to illustrate depression and mania. Older children might read some of the same basic literature that is put out for patients. Your parents might know the term "manic-depression" rather than "bipolar," though they may not truly understand what that means. Try to discuss things in ways that make sense to them.

Allow your children, even if they are still young, to help you when they can. Start teaching them to do chores around the house, pick up after themselves and entertain themselves when you need to get things done.

If the children are school-aged or teens, they can be a lot of help and can learn to give and ask for reality checks when they need them. Never turn a child, even an adult child, into a confidante with issues in your marriage. This puts them in a difficult position between two parents.

It is possible that your parents and in-laws will not understand or will not accept that there is mental illness in the family. You have to feel your way around that and decide exactly how much to tell them and how much help or what type of help to expect from them. Generally, you can expect limited help. You might get a grandma to babysit once in a while so that you can go with your spouse to an appointment with the psychiatrist. You might even ask for babysitting so that you can take a day away and clear your head.

Be careful what you tell friends and extended family. You may end up with a lot of great moral support, but you might also end up with a lot of unwanted and inappropriate advice. If it is just going to make everyone uncomfortable, try to get the help you need without telling too much of the story. Stick to simple facts.

Don't keep the mental illness a secret—that just makes it seem more important and confuses anyone who knows something is wrong—just limit your discussions. Tell what you need and why as simply and as precisely as possible. Avoid whining to family and friends—it doesn't make a good impression and it won't get you anywhere.

If you find yourself wanting to vent about the damage bipolar disorder has done to your marriage and your life, join a support group or find a therapist and vent to people who actually understand.

Telling your story to people who don't understand it will just make everyone nervous about being near you and your spouse. You might get some sympathy, but you'll lose friendships if people can't take it.

You may have learned to do everything yourself and the control of doing that can be pretty heady, but unless you have an endless supply of energy, a little help will do wonders. Think about the ways that people can help you and start asking.

While there are some people who will be happy just to be of assistance, do not assume that everyone will feel that way. Make sure there is something "in it" for them when at all possible.

While family members might jump at the chance to spend time with your children, they may not always be available when you need them. Have a back-up plan. The neighbors may watch your children while you attend appointments if you can take their children from time to time.

Children may be willing to pick up after dinner if it means that the whole family will be able to go to the park or do some other fun activity together.

You may find that there are tasks you can trade with a friend that will make both of your lives easier—mowing two lawns, throwing in extra loads of laundry, even making large meals and trading the "leftovers" can give you both a chance to help and be helped.

You may find that you can pay for help when you need it. There are some tasks that require a specialist and others that nobody wants to do unless they are getting paid. Ask friends and neighbors for recommendations and avoid signing any sort of long-term contract until you know that you have found the right person for the job.

Perhaps as you go through the list, you will find things that your spouse is willing and able to do, but that you hadn't discussed because it's just always been your job. My husband usually does the cooking these days because he has time and generally enjoys doing it. I would never have suggested it myself, but he offered when I was obviously overwhelmed and it's been working for us ever since.

Think outside the box.

Assistance Team Plan

Make a list of the things that you need help with—the things that your spouse can't do because of the disorder, or things you don't have the time or energy to do. Also include things that would just be helpful to have done for you, even if you really could do them yourself.

Also make a list of people who might be available or willing to help; these are your team members, whether they help on a consistent basis or just occasionally. Consider what you might be willing to pay—in money or favors—for these tasks. Work on matching up the tasks with the team members and start asking.

Task I need help with	Team member	In exchange I can

Now You Are Ready To Help Others

If you've ever tried to help a child who had fallen into deep water, you have an idea of what it's like to help someone with bipolar disorder. Your spouse may desperately want your help, but be so busy thrashing about and trying to fix things that it becomes nearly impossible for you to do anything helpful. You might very well be hurt in the process.

It may be impossible to help someone in the throes of mania—short of dragging an unwilling patient to the hospital or calling the police. (The men in white coats don't actually come out any more, if they ever really did.) At one time I was told that it was negligent and dangerous not to call the police if my husband got out of control. Although this was not true at that time and place, it is something you have to think about and get some local information ahead of time to know what your options are realistically.

In some areas when you call the emergency number and tell them that a person is mentally ill, they will send out a team that is trained to deal with mental health issues. In other areas, they send out the police who are rarely trained for this type of situation. They can seriously complicate matters or shoot someone who doesn't need or deserve to be shot.

I have always lived in areas without access to a mental health assessment team and I'd rather deal with the problem myself than to get people involved who know nothing about the situation and have easy access to deadly force, but my husband has never been in a violent mood with access to a weapon, either. Before you reach a crisis situation, find out what kind of help is available and know the number to call when you need it.

The best time to start to get help is when the person who needs help KNOWS that help is needed. Look for depressions. Manic people are generally unaware that there is a problem. Depressed people want and need help.

Unfortunately, they are often able to get the wrong kind of help. Never send a depressed person with bipolar disorder to the doctor alone no matter what. Depressed people with bipolar disorder can usually talk a doctor into giving them anti-depressant drugs. Anti-depressant drugs may be used to treat depression, but if they are taken without a mood stabilizing drug of some sort—whether it's an actual mood stabilizer like lithium or an anti-psychotic—without that balancing drug you will have front row seats to a show you don't want to see.

It is rare indeed that anti-depressants or stimulants can be given to a person with bipolar disorder without triggering a manic episode. Even in people with bipolar 2, the form with no true mania, you can see a drug-induced mania. Trust me; you don't want to see this.

How do I know that? Both my husband, who has bipolar 1, and my son (diagnosed with ADHD), have suffered drug induced mania. It was not a pretty sight. If your spouse is in a receptive mood, agree that this is a team project, go together to meet with a doctor and make sure the doctor knows all sides of the story before writing a prescription.

There are many situations that come up and many possible responses. Some will work for most people, while some will work for a few people. Unfortunately, none of them will work for everyone, so you just have to learn as much as possible about your own situation and make an educated guess about which tactics are likely to work for you.

If you don't like trial and error, join the club. No one does, but even the doctors are often left with this as their only option in this disorder—nothing works for everyone and sometimes the most logical response is the wrong one. This is not a rational or logical disorder.

Doctors, Drugs and Therapy

We're all in this together—working as a team is the best chance you have for dealing successfully with bipolar disorder.

What kind of doctor do you see if you have bipolar disorder? Are all psychiatrists pretty much the same? What about psychologists and therapists? Can the family doctor treat bipolar disorder?

Legally, the family doctor can prescribe the medications needed to control bipolar disorder. Any physician can order the tests to measure blood levels and to watch for toxicity. But this is a very difficult and complicated disorder and many family practice doctors would not be comfortable treating it.

If you are in an area where there are no specialists or if you don't have insurance to cover specialists, the family doctor may be willing to work with you.

If location or insurance limits your options to one or two psychiatrists who do not have the specialized knowledge or philosophy that you are looking for, you have to work with what you have. You need that source of prescription medication and there is no way around it.

Since your spouse needs a bipolar specialist of some sort, you may have to become that specialist. You will need to buy books, go online and do research, join the National Association for the Mentally Ill (NAMI) and any other support group you can find, and be prepared to educate the doctor. You will have to do this politely and humbly, but you can do it.

You should be aware that specialists may have their opinions colored by their specialty. Each doctor may see something different and getting an accurate diagnosis and correct treatment can be tricky. The diagnostic manual for mental health is little more than a list that matches symptoms to "disorders" with a tremendous amount of overlap.

A psychiatrist might feel that problems can be solved with medication. Most will admit that talk therapy can be helpful, but they are more inclined to diagnose chemical imbalance, something they studied, than a personality disorder. There may be significant overlap of symptoms although treatment can be very different. It is important to have a doctor or team of doctors who are interested in sorting it all out.

Many talk therapists will see personality disorders instead of chemical imbalances because that is what they have studied and the differences may be hard to see, especially if they are only meeting for one hour when the patient is on "company" behavior or actively trying to manipulate the therapist. The differences are in the minute details that won't show up.

Having both types of specialist makes it more likely that all sides will be explored. As hard as it is to get a diagnosis, you don't want to be stuck with a wrong diagnosis or treating just part of the disorder.

It might be best to work with someone who specializes in diagnosing mental illnesses to get the diagnosis and then move on to someone who treats the disorder that is diagnosed.

Psychiatrists

The first specialist you need to find is a psychiatrist who has experience, preferably successful experience, working with patients with bipolar disorder.

If you are calling a list of doctors, ask open ended questions. Not "Have you treated bipolar disorder?" but "What is your specialty?" or "What types of disorder have you treated successfully?" Listen carefully to the answers. You will find the right one faster with more information.

If you ask about bipolar, a doctor who has one bipolar patient will say "yes." If the doctor doesn't mention bipolar or mood disorders then bipolar is probably not a specialty. Keep looking.

Ask if family involvement is encouraged. Doctors can talk a good talk about the patient needing to take responsibility for treatment, but people with serious mental illnesses need a lot of help in handling that responsibility—even an alcoholic in AA gets a sponsor.

Any psychiatrist that doesn't welcome input from a family member should be passed by for one who does. There may be illnesses and degrees of illness that a doctor can handle with the patient alone, but bipolar disorder is too tricky for that.

I have yet to hear of people with bipolar who can accurately report on their own progress consistently. With a little luck, they might be able to describe how they are feeling today. Remembering how they have been doing last week or in the weeks since the last appointment, and describing that accurately, well, that task is hard enough for a mentally healthy person. Bipolar affects the memory. This is a known symptom.

People in a hypo-manic state might be feeling really good today and not even consider mentioning that they have just come out of a depression, a manic episode, or some other troubled state. If today is not absolutely typical of the time between appointments, the doctor isn't likely to hear about it.

If meds were missed just before a mood swing, it is possible that the patient won't make the connection—so the doctor won't know about it. In fact, if a change is noticed, chances are pretty good that the doctor won't be able to get enough information to know whether the current meds are working and missed doses contributed to any problems, or the meds are basically working but some event contributed to the mood change and an adjustment might be needed, or the meds aren't working at all and need to be changed more dramatically.

Lack of insight is so common as to be considered a symptom. How much help is someone who doesn't think it's abnormal to spend 22 hours a day in bed, to forgo normal hygiene for weeks on end or to spend the whole night, literally the whole night, arguing about something that nobody even cares about?

There are no physical signs, no blood tests, no X-rays, that offer much help in choosing meds for a bipolar patient—all you have is behavior and the patients' descriptions. Under the circumstances, even a mind reader wouldn't get very far. Any doctor who thinks it's best to treat the patient without considering any information that can be gathered from friends and family either has an extraordinarily high opinion of his or her skills or just plain doesn't understand this disorder.

And even if you have this genius doctor who can tell just by looking at patients whether they need a bit more mood stabilizer or a little less anti-depressant, you need to hear it directly from the doctor. Someone who can remember what the doctor said, even after the whole ride home, needs to know which meds are for what and which meds can be safely adjusted and by how much and in what situation. If there is a serious reaction, can we just omit this med or do we call right away or go to the hospital or what?

If poor memory is a normal symptom of bipolar (and it is), then expecting the patient to remember medication instructions, especially to remember what to do when something has gone wrong and panic sets in, well, it just isn't a realistic expectation.

Psychologists and Therapists

It is usually best to work with medications to get some stability before speaking with a talk therapist, but sometimes a good therapist can help a person work through issues that prevent him or her from accepting a diagnosis or taking appropriate medication. A therapist or psychologist who is skilled at working with such issues might be instrumental in getting a person into appropriate medical treatment.

Look for a talk therapist who knows about bipolar disorder and who can work with the psychiatrist. A therapist should not be discussing a patient with anyone else—confidentiality is absolutely necessary for this type of treatment—but it would be nice if the therapist is willing to listen to the concerns of family members to get a more balanced view. A therapist who welcomes a spouse or family member to attend part of a session from time to time may be ideal if that is alright with your spouse.

Once a person is stabilized with medication, a therapist will help the patient to understand what the diagnosis means. The therapist can help with coping skills and with learning to recognize the feelings that precipitate a mood change so that action can be taken to prevent episodes.

A therapist can also help sort out what to tell the psychiatrist to help with treatment. Because the therapist usually spends much more time with a patient than a psychiatrist, he or she may be able to help the patient to express concerns more efficiently so the psychiatrist has a better idea of what is going on.

Having two different doctors—a therapist and a psychiatrist—is the most effective course of therapy, because a psychiatrist will see things that can be improved with medication and a therapist will see things that can be improved with training and therapy.

By the time a person is diagnosed with bipolar, a combination of other issues has usually materialized and both specialists are necessary to sort them out.

It is important to keep accurate records. This is essential in helping the doctors that are treating this disorder to know what is working, what isn't working, and what problems or complications they are dealing with. To that end, a mood diary with as much detail as possible is a useful tool.

Mood Charts

You can work on these together or keep separate charts and compare.

There are many types of mood chart available from the Internet, from other books, or from your psychiatrist or therapist. Use the one that seems the most helpful for you or create one of your own.

Do not take this on as a permanent additional responsibility. Use it as a tool to watch for patterns and to show the doctor the effects of medications and triggers. If you are marking the same information every day for weeks on end, you can probably put it away until there is a change.

Keeping a journal with details of specific events may help, but marking a mood chart every evening or every time the mood changes—in cases where moods last longer—will also be useful in telling if something needs to be changed.

The additional information a journal might include could be invaluable, but unless you are very disciplined and determined, it is unlikely that you will be able to make the time to write much unless it is already a part of your schedule.

A checkmark on a chart is a fairly quick and easy way to track the swings of bipolar—something you might be able to find time for on a regular basis.

Another alternative is to use a regular calendar and a code: numbers 1-10 for mood, with 1 being very depressed and 10 being fully manic and a letter for any triggers or changes: M=medication issue, R=change in routines, D=change in diet, S=change in sleep, A=change in activity level, and anything else that seems useful for you.

Triggers/Changes

	Sunday	Monday	Tuesday	Wednesday	Thursday	Friday	Saturday
Meds Missed /Not taken on time.							
Change in Routines							
Change in Diet							
Change in Sleep Habits							
Change in Activity Level							
Other Therapy _____							
Other Stressors _____							

Moods

	Sunday	Monday	Tuesday	Wednesday	Thursday	Friday	Saturday
Manic							
Hypo-Manic							
Normal (?)							
Mixed							
Mild Depression							
Depressed							

Books

Loving Someone With Bipolar Disorder by Julie A. Fast and John D. Preston. I have only skimmed this book by an author who, along with her partner, has been diagnosed with bipolar disorder. Lots of treatment and lifestyle ideas. Some complain that it makes the partner into a caregiver and the disorder a central component, but until there is successful treatment in place, that's just the way it is.

The Bipolar Disorder Survival Guide: What You and Your Family Need to Know by David J. Miklowitz, PhD. is written from the perspective of a Professor of Psychology who has also written a professional resource book *Bipolar Disorder: A Family-Focused Treatment Approach.* The book is intended for the bipolar patient as well as the family.

Medication Simplified

There are a number of psychiatric medications that are used to treat bipolar disorder. Knowing what they are and what they do makes you a more valuable member of the treatment

Remember, there is no cure. Any discussion of taking medications for a few weeks or months and then discontinuing them should include the doctor. When medication is discontinued, symptoms will come back, sometimes slowly, other times suddenly. You and your partner will soon be in the same position as if no medication had ever been used, which may be a pretty dramatic change.

If you are tempted to try a more natural approach, remember that there is nothing natural about the brain chemistry in bipolar disorder—in fact, the bipolar brain seems to work about the same as any other brain when compromised by mind-altering drugs. Bipolar is a chemical disorder—even if it is triggered by nonchemical triggers—and the most efficient treatment is chemical, combined with healthy lifestyle changes that help to keep the brain from producing more destabilizing chemicals.

All psychiatric medications have side effects and overdoses can be dangerous. Most take at least a few days, some a few weeks or more, to get to a therapeutic level in the blood. Some side effects start immediately and will diminish with time, so even though it seems like the only effects are bad ones at first, if possible you should allow some time to adjust to a new medication before giving up.

Make sure you ask the doctor about any specific side effects that might be serious. You may also need to try different dosages and combinations, so don't dismiss a specific medication after one trial unless it causes serious side effects. Some side effects that seem serious are known to disappear or decrease in time. Other side effects that might seem just annoying might be the first signs of a deadly reaction.

There are three categories of medication that are commonly used to treat the symptoms of bipolar disorder. Anti-depressants are used to treat depression. Anti-psychotics are used to treat psychotic features of mania. Mood stabilizers are used to hold the moods closer to the center and to avoid both extremes.

Mood Stabilizers

Some psychiatrists will avoid the use of mood stabilizers (MS) and some patients will refuse to use them because it means that "something is seriously wrong," but they are the backbone of successful treatment of bipolar disorder. Mood stabilizers can be used alone or in combination with other types of medication.

Some mood stabilizers are also used for other purposes—some are anti-seizure medications and the mood stabilizing property is an "off-label, not FDA approved" use. This does not mean that they don't work for this purpose, but that they haven't gone through the process to be approved. Doctors use them because they know that they work in some cases when "approved" drugs don't. An added benefit of these medications and those with multiple approvals is that it keeps the pharmacy and guests who peak in your medicine cabinet guessing.

We really don't know what makes them work, but we know how these drugs affect most people and there are two different types of mood stabilizers.

1. Lithium and Depakote (and a few others) are used to create milder mood swings. You may still notice mood changes—from mild mania to mild or moderate depression—but the swings will be less pronounced and the symptoms less disruptive than before medication. Blood levels of these drugs must be watched closely because therapeutic levels and toxic levels tend to be close.

2. Lamictal is a newer type of mood stabilizer that seems to create more stability between mood swings. While it does not necessarily make episodes more bearable, it may provide some rest between episodes. This could be a lifesaver if the moods change on a dime and you both need time to recover.

Anti-psychotics

Antipsychotic (AP) medications are used to control the manic episodes that occur in bipolar 1. They are used to treat racing thoughts, agitation, delusions and other symptoms of mania.

Typical anti-psychotic medications, such as Haldol and Compazine are usually used in the most serious cases in a hospital setting. These potent drugs can bring a person out of an episode fairly quickly, but they must be handled very carefully.

Atypical anti-psychotic medications are more commonly used for long-term control. Abilify, Risperadol, Zyprexa, and Geodon are atypical antipsychotic medications that are commonly used to treat bipolar mania. Some of these seem to have mood stabilizing properties for some patients, but it's strictly a trial and error proposition and errors can be pretty frightening.

Although taking an antipsychotic medication might seem to indicate that a person tends to be psychotic, most of the atypical antipsychotic medications also have other uses, so don't be too concerned that they are in your medicine cabinet. It is always better to have anti-psychotics in the medicine cabinet than a psychotic person in the house.

Anti-depressants

Anti-depressants (AD) can bring an end to a depressive episode or prevent one from happening. They can ameliorate the symptoms of a depressive episode if one does happen. Unfortunately, they can also trigger a manic episode in a person with bipolar disorder. Anti-depressants should ALWAYS be balanced with mood stabilizers and possibly antipsychotic medications in cases of bipolar disorder.

The current thought is that anti-depressants really don't do much for bipolar depression and, because of the risk of triggering mania, should be avoided entirely in favor of physical exercise or certain supplements (notably Omega-3). Because getting a depressed person to exercise is nothing short of a miracle (at least at my house) anti-depressants are a popular alternative, if only for the placebo effect.

If a doctor ever prescribes unopposed anti-depressants (or stimulants) to your bipolar spouse, make sure you get a detailed description of what you need to do when mania ensues. Sometimes bringing this up to the doctor will get you a change in the prescription order.

Some anti-depressant drugs are billed as "safe" for bipolar patients, but don't let the doctor talk you into using these alone to treat bipolar—safe is a relative term and the doctor isn't going home with you. Insist on something to balance these meds or the doctor's cell number on your speed dial. Ok, not terribly practical, but we have been there and I wouldn't wish that on anyone.

There are a lot of anti-depressants and many of them have alternate uses that might help the doctor decide which one to prescribe. Some help with sleep, others help with anxiety and some even help with certain types of headaches. My husband was on one that is commonly used under a different name to help people stop smoking. If one of the side effects is that it helps with another problem the patient is experiencing, well, that has to be a good thing.

At some point it may be brought up that an anti-depressant might help you to deal with some of the complexities of your life. People who do not have bipolar disorder can take antidepressants alone. If the stress is getting to you, if you are feeling hopeless or helpless or angry or sad or whatever and the doctor suggests a prescription, by all means give it a try. Situational depression (depression that is caused by a hard situation) can turn into chronic or major depression if it is prolonged and untreated.

You may have to try two or three different medications before you find one that works. Don't take it as a personal failure if you need help. What kind of example are you setting if you say "there's nothing wrong with taking mind altering drugs if your mind needs altering" to your spouse while refusing to do it for yourself.

Make a list of the medications your spouse is taking and look them up in a current drug manual (*Physicians' Desk Reference*) or online to determine the class of drugs. You might be surprised at what some of them are used for besides bipolar disorder.

Watch for changes in behavior with medication changes and be prepared to discuss behavior that concerns you with your spouse and the psychiatrist. Include medications that are prescribed by other doctors and check for interactions or side effects to discuss with the doctors. This is for your convenience and to help you make your case if you feel something is wrong. Use it as needed.

Medication	MS	AP	AD	Other uses:

Medication Books

Clinical Psychopharmacology Made Ridiculously Simple by John Preston. Unfortunately, anything about psych meds is obsolete before printing. New drugs come out all the time, but if you want something to help you sort out the meds, this should help. It is best if you can talk to the psychiatrist with a sound understanding of what these drugs can do.

http://www.crazymeds.us/ is our favorite web site for psychiatric medication information. It is also helpful to look up the official web site of the drug company that makes each medication for full prescribing information.

A simple search on the name of the drug will bring up a number of resources—while the drug companies do want to sell drugs, they have to protect themselves from liability, so they stick pretty close to the truth that they can prove. Other sites may have a less obvious objective and may lean heavily on rumors and a few strange cases. Beware.

The most recent version of the *Physicians' Desk Reference* is also a good source of information on prescription medication. It is written for doctors, so there is a lot of medical terminology and information that doesn't apply to your specific situation. Psychiatric medications are not well understood, so the information in the book will change with each edition as new discoveries are made.

Support Stability

Please remain seated and keep hands and
feet inside the car until the ride comes to
a complete stop.

There will be times when even the best combination of medications will fall short and some stressor will trigger an episode. You may have to call the psychiatrist to get the meds adjusted, or you may have to duck and run to protect yourself.

Supporting stability may sound simple—of course you want to do everything in your power to support stability—but sometimes it is impossible to know what will help and what will make matters worse.

One possible method to avoid the damage of an episode is something I call the three Ds: Detach, Distract, and Defuse. You learned about detaching in chapter 3, and besides helping you cope, it also helps you to remain calm enough to proceed with any of the tactics you might learn. Once you are speaking and thinking calmly, you can work out your strategy to Distract—hey, look, there's a hummingbird at the feeder! Shhhhhhhhh, does that sound like water dripping? From there you can move on to Defuse—Honey, I know this is a serious discussion, but I'm just too emotional right now to handle it, can we talk about this tomorrow when I've had time to calm down and think it through? (Keep the blame on your own emotions or you're likely to start another round.)

Having lived this life and having listened to people who have bipolar disorder, I have come up with a few ideas of what to do—and what not to do, even if it seems natural and helpful at the time.

Beware the Maniac

When mania takes over, it can seem like a scene from a bad horror movie. The mild-mannered victim suddenly becomes a raving monster. Nothing you do is right and the whole world is out to "get" your partner. These strategies can minimize your stress during a manic episode:

1. Do not try to argue logically. Logic and rational arguments will get you nowhere and will just irritate your spouse. People with bipolar disorder are not capable of thinking rationally while in episode.

2. Do not give in to something you feel strongly about. Spending a set dollar amount at the local thrift shop might satisfy the urge to splurge, but blowing the rent on a great pair of jeans or a new tool for a hobby will do too much damage in the long run.

3. Choose your battles. You don't have the energy to fight over every bad decision someone can make during a manic episode. You can make it clear how you feel about each decision, but let the small ones slide and save your energy for the important stuff.

4. Find things you can agree with. It may be stretching things, but agreeing, even in the smallest way, can help to defuse a dangerous situation.

5. Do not become agitated yourself. If you can stay calm, speak slowly and clearly, think before you act or speak, and avoid direct confrontations, you may not be able to calm your spouse, but you will help keep others in the house calm and you will be a much more believable witness if you have to call the doctor or police.

6. Call the doctor and explain what is happening in as much detail as possible. If manic episodes are expected, have the doctor prescribe a medication to be taken at the start of an episode as

needed. (The prescription bottle may say "PRN" which is doctor-speak for "as needed")

7. Gently suggest that the medication the doctor has prescribed in case of mania might help with symptoms that bother your spouse. While mania may not be totally unpleasant for the patient, there are some symptoms that are troublesome—racing thoughts, compulsive behaviors, paranoia, insomnia, etc.

8. Gently suggest a calming activity. "Take a hike" is not a gentle suggestion. "Would you like me to run you a nice warm bath?" or "Do you want to go with me when I walk the dog?" is a gentle suggestion. Even those can get you into trouble sometimes.

9. Do not talk down to a person in episode. Even without delusions of grandeur, such things only irritate people and such irritations aggravate manic symptoms. Speak calmly and clearly— no baby talk, no simple rational explanations and no emotional pleas.

10. Don't expect miracles. Nothing you do will cure mania. Even the experts, with serious drugs in their bag of tricks, take time to get an episode under control. Medications that leave a person stiff and silent may have an immediate effect, but it's not the desired effect. You can get immediate results in many ways, but these are not the results we want.

It's Just the Depression Talking

When depression is running my house it's usually pretty subdued. In fact, it is a major effort to get out of bed in the afternoon (morning? What's morning?) or to put forth the slightest effort. If your spouse is more active at this time, you may have to worry about suicide or other acts of self-destruction. These strategies can minimize your stress during a depressive episode:

1. Do not try to argue rationally. If the world is out to get you, hearing that things aren't really so bad or that you are over-reacting is not helpful. Platitudes are irritating.

2. Do not give in to something that you feel strongly about. If you have to do things alone, do them alone. Don't cancel your social schedule—it may just make you want to join in the depression. Have fun when you can.

3. Choose your battles. It is more important to guard health and safety than to worry about details. If all the moping gets you down, get yourself out. You can't make a depressed person be less negative, but you can look for something positive for yourself.

4. Find things you agree with that are neutral. Agreeing that the world is a lousy place might seem logical at some point, but that tends to feed the depression monster. Agree that chicken looks good for dinner or that "we have to do something about this depression."

5. Do not become depressed yourself. This is probably the easiest and hardest piece of advice because it seems pretty self-evident, but it's harder than it looks. It's hard to live with a person with depression and it can make you sad to think about your future together. Two steps further and you're sliding downhill.

6. Call the doctor and describe as accurately as possible what is going on. Sleep patterns, quotes, activity levels, and choice of activities are clues that help the doctor determine what changes need to be made. Becoming emotional yourself will not work and will give you less credibility with most doctors.

7. Gently suggest that depression might be an issue and talk about adjusting medications according to what you may have discussed with the doctor at an earlier time.

8. Gently suggest some very minor form of exercise. Although the last thing a person with depression will want to do is exercise, it is one of the few things, besides medication, that can have a positive effect. Asking for help with a physical activity—no matter how trivial—is a step in the right direction. "Can you hold the bag while I rake the leaves in?" gets you both out of the house and doing something constructive.

9. Put on a funny movie. Although the Three Stooges might just give dangerous ideas to a person in mania, laughter is an exercise that comes relatively easy and is incredibly positive. Choose something that is hopelessly silly or a favorite of your spouse to avoid continued griping and whining.

10. Don't expect miracles. Eating, walking around or laughing at a movie may provide some small temporary relief, but there is no magic cure for depression.

There are a lot of effective non-chemical treatments that can be used in addition to appropriate medication and that don't take a lot of your time, money, or strength. Learning which of those are most useful to your spouse may take time—it is always trial and error with this disorder—but can prove worthwhile when an episode is getting you down.

Remember, none of these ideas will work miracles with someone who is not appropriately medicated, but they may help and are not likely to make matters any worse.

Personalized Action Plan

Use this chart to plan specific actions to take when you see symptoms that an episode is starting or when one is in progress and you are too stressed to think it through.

When I notice:	I will:
(example) Increased activity	Keep an eye on the bank accounts.

Is It Really Just the Bipolar?

Whether you're dealing with the simplest case of bipolar disorder or a multiple- diagnosis addictive personality, there will be times when you think: Ok, is this part of the disorder or am I married to a jerk? Keep in mind that this is not an either /or situation.

If you've read through the book definition of bipolar disorder and some authoritative articles on the symptoms and diagnosis of bipolar disorder, you may be pretty confused. I know I was and, after three years in "the system," I am still working on figuring it all out. I can't really share what I don't know, but I'll give you the standard listing of symptoms that we've all read and tell you how those symptoms look in real people—my husband and the family members of people in my support groups.

If you get a bit squeamish about sex or violence, you might want to grab a cup of coffee or a glass of wine before we get into it. Go ahead and get that now. I didn't say half a chocolate cake and a pint of Hagen Das! Fine, just don't get sticky on my book.

Symptoms of Bipolar

I am taking a list from WebMD.com, though I could have copied a nearly identical list from any number of sources:

The primary symptoms of bipolar disorder are dramatic and unpredictable mood swings. The illness has two strongly contrasting phases.

In the manic phase:
Euphoria or irritability
Excessive talk; racing thoughts
Inflated self-esteem
Unusual energy; less need for sleep
Impulsiveness, a reckless pursuit of gratification -- shopping sprees, impetuous travel, more and sometimes promiscuous sex, high-risk business investments, fast driving
Hallucinations and or delusions

In the depressive phase:
Depressed mood and low self-esteem
Low energy levels and apathy
Sadness, loneliness, helplessness, guilt
Slow speech, fatigue, and poor coordination
Insomnia or oversleeping
Suicidal thoughts and feelings
Poor concentration
Lack of interest or pleasure in usual activities

OK, starting from the beginning, we all know what mood swings are, but when we first saw that swing from depression to mania or from mania to depression, we probably didn't think of it as a mood swing. We thought we were losing our own minds. We thought the body snatchers had grabbed our loved one. We may have been aware of an event that might affect our spouse's mood, but not "like that!" Having seen or experienced PMS doesn't begin to prepare you for this kind of mood swing.

That's what a bipolar mood swing looks like. We may learn to accept the changes as mood swings, but they never fail to astonish us and catch us off guard. That's the nature of bipolar mood swings.

How do you know it's bipolar and not something else? Bipolar mood swings often have little, if anything, to do with real life situations. A person with bipolar mood swings is up or down for no apparent reason. The swings are also much more pronounced than they would be in a healthy person. Bipolar moods are not happy or sad, they are bouncing off the wall and floating on a cloud, or the world is coming to an end and I hate my life.

Teenagers have mood swings that are similar to bipolar mood swings in that they are chemically induced (raging hormones), but they are also triggered by situations, such as grades, bullies and friends. Although they may seem to be dramatic overreactions, they do make sense to other teenagers.

Bipolar mood swings have much less basis in experience. The mood is dramatically out of proportion to the situation or there seems to be no reason. I know, teenagers are the same way sometimes, trust me, there is a big difference. When you actually see it you'll know something is wrong.

The symptoms of mania:

Euphoria or irritability. When diagnosing mania most people look for the euphoria. Irritability could mean anything, but unexplained euphoria is a symptom of mania. Unfortunately, euphoria is less common, and may only be seen during certain stages of mania or not at all. It is often more helpful to look for unexplained irritability. If someone is snapping at you suddenly in a situation where usually that person would not be upset, that's irritability and it could be a symptom of mania. Don't get me wrong, it could also mean that they aren't feeling well for any number of reasons and are more sensitive, so look for other symptoms, too. But if a person is diagnosed with bipolar and is behaving in an irritable manner, consider the possibility that they may be manic or on the way into mania. Watch for other symptoms.

For example, my husband is usually amused by the antics of all sorts of animals, including pets, but this morning he was yelling at a puppy for "scaring" away his hummingbirds. Forget that before the birds flew away, they were swooping at the pup to get a better look and that she was just standing there watching, while he was making loud noises yelling at the dog which is much more likely to bother the little birds. In this case "irritable" means angry for no apparent reason or a reason that makes no sense.

Excessive talking or racing thoughts. Some people talk fast all of the time, but when a person with bipolar is ramping up—going manic—their speech may become much faster than what is normal for them. They may seem to be trying to keep up with thoughts that are moving too fast for speech, or they may complain of racing thoughts. If your strong, silent type turns into Chatty Cathy, mania is on the horizon.

Inflated self-esteem. There are plenty of people with bipolar disorder who are smarter, stronger, or more beautiful, but while in mania, they may believe that they are the smartest, strongest, best. They may believe they are gods or that they have a special mission from God, that they are chosen, special in some way. Lots of people can be a bit arrogant, but we are talking about someone who goes from "nobody loves me" to "stay off the phone; the President may be trying to call for my opinion on the war." If it doesn't seem that extreme to you, get yourself a reality check and see what other people think. This is the kind of thing that can sneak up on you and have you half-believing the stories.

Unusual energy or less need for sleep. Pulling an all-nighter before an exam may be normal. Spending the whole night running around the house, cleaning, organizing, remodeling or doing other tasks for which there is no specific deadline—and being able to do it night after night with little or no rest—that's mania.

Impulsiveness or a reckless pursuit of gratification -- Shopping sprees, impetuous travel, more and sometimes promiscuous sex, high-risk business investments and fast driving are ways this symptom presents. These things are skimmed over in most books, but they are usually the symptoms that cause the most trouble and bring people into treatment. When people with bipolar disorder exhibit this symptom, it might be seen as criminal activity, compulsive behavior or simple lack of impulse control, but it is actually more complicated.

People at certain levels of mania are not capable of anticipating consequences of their actions or even comprehending that their actions have consequences. Let me repeat that: while in a manic episode, individuals do not have any comprehension of cause and effect, that actions have consequences, that what they do affects anyone else or that it can change the future. It simply doesn't occur to them.

There are two more specific symptoms that are common and that tend to get skimmed over by doctors that are devastating to families. Those symptoms are hyper-sexuality (oversexed) and profligacy (overspending). While these symptoms are not universal, they are common enough and destructive enough to be worth considering individually.

Hyper-sexuality may simply be a stronger interest in appropriate sexual activity, but it can lead to requests to engage in more frequent, more risky, and more bizarre sex acts. When Troy is ramping up, he seems sexually interested in anything in a skirt, but as far as I know, he has always come home to act out his fantasies. I'm generally happy to go along, though a person does need to sleep sometimes and some of the stuff has been a bit much even for me.

It is not uncommon for a person suffering from hyper-sexuality to go outside the marriage relationship—to pornography, prostitutes or affairs—to satisfy their urges. Whether you can forgive this sort of behavior really depends on you and on the situation. A person with abnormal sexual urges does not HAVE to give in to them. It's still a choice. It's still cheating.

If you want to forgive and go on with the marriage, make sure you get all of the appropriate testing for STDs done—there's some pretty nasty stuff out there—and set boundaries that will keep you physically safe. You also need to get into some form of marriage counseling for this. Without it your partner is likely to repeat these behaviors and you will build resentments, not knowing quite where to draw the line. This is a boundary that will help keep you emotionally safe.

Profligacy. I had to find this term myself because it doesn't appear in the medical literature that I've seen. The wasteful, extravagant, without-a-thought-to-paying-debts mentality is almost a defining characteristic of bipolar mania. The jokes about what has come to the door via eBay are no accident. People with bipolar disorder really have no thought of consequences when it comes to ordering things online or buying things in a store while they are in an episode. They just think of the immediate gratification of possessing whatever it is that they desire at the moment.

Hallucinations or delusions. These are another dead giveaway that don't happen nearly as often as people seem to expect or, at least, are not reported as often as you'd expect. There are people who keep their hallucinations or delusions hidden. They don't tell people that they hear voices or try to explain what they believe or think. If you do discover that a person is hearing voices, seeing things that aren't there, or trusting beliefs that have no basis in fact, call a doctor immediately or go to the emergency room—this can be serious. But if these things never happen, don't assume that it's not serious or that it's not real bipolar. This is just one of many possible symptoms.

Paranoia is one type of false belief that may occur and provoke violence—self defense from a perceived threat that no one else can see. Other false beliefs can be as varied as the people who have them. Strange fears, strange lack of fear or ideas about special gifts or abilities, may be mentioned or may be discovered through behavior.

In the depressive phase:

Depressed mood and low self-esteem. The person who thinks he's God's gift or God Himself when manic can believe that he doesn't deserve to live when depressed. Same person, no real change in situation, just a bit of mood cycling and you get an opposite assessment.

Low energy levels and apathy. Again, a person who didn't seem to need sleep may seem to be making up for lost sleep. There are rocks that have more energy.

Sadness, loneliness, helplessness and guilt. It might seem that some of this is a natural response to the manic behavior—shouldn't they be sad and guilty when they've done things that risk their lives, their finances and their relationships? Perhaps, but not to this degree and not without having some understanding of what they have done.

It would be nice if there was a real repenting from irresponsible manic behavior, but this sadness and guilt are often totally unrelated to the mania. Usually there is either no reason for these feelings or the reason that is given is not related to what has actually been happening.

There may also be a tendency to try to share these feelings, to spread around the guilt, loneliness, sadness and helplessness by blaming you for everything that has ever gone wrong in the world.

This can be a pretty convincing argument—remember, this is depression talking. It is hard to tell if someone is making things up on the fly when the person actually believes them, which is often the case. Note to self: You are not personally responsible for original sin.

Slow speech, fatigue and poor coordination. People in a bipolar depressive state may tend to do everything as if in a movie in slow motion. If you start doing things for them because they seem so slow, they will probably let you and get even slower and more lethargic. Look the other way if you have to, but make them do as much as they will for themselves or you'll be doing everything. Give yourself a break.

Insomnia or oversleeping. During depression this may be the first clue that something is wrong. Getting the right amount of sleep every night is a big part of staying mentally and emotionally healthy and if someone is suddenly sleeping half the day—whether or not they are up during the night—it is a fairly positive sign of depression. The insomnia is different from the bouncing around all night long of mania. It's more the "so tired I can't sleep," irritable, "don't breath so loud" kind of insomnia.

Suicidal thoughts and feelings. These are more than a casual "I hate my job, I wish I were dead" kind of thing. There may be actual plans being worked out in the mind and even an attempt. Take this seriously because even a lame attempt can succeed.

Poor concentration. This could mean a drop in productivity at work or home. When a person can't concentrate on anything long enough to make it make sense, it can be pretty frightening as well as being a threat to any sort of success.

Lack of interest or pleasure in usual activities. This may not mean that the person won't show some interest or enthusiasm over something good, but it will all be under reaction. A trip to Hawaii will be met with the type of enthusiasm generally reserved for the ugly Father's Day tie or the underwear under the Christmas tree.

There are a lot of reasons that you might see symptoms of mania or depression in a normal healthy person, but not to the degree that you'll see them in a person with bipolar disorder.

Normal people go through periods of extreme productivity when they get excited about a project or idea and later go through periods of depression when they finish the project and are thinking "is that all there is?" or when they realize that whatever they have accomplished is not going to change the world in the way they might have hoped.

They also have depressive episodes when they think about the evil in the world and how helpless we, as individual human beings, are to fight it. If you look closely, you will see that these "mood swings" are directly related to situations and make a certain amount of sense— even if they are exaggerations.

A person "in love" will sometimes appear manic, as will someone who has just achieved some dream, but a person without a mood disorder will remain rational on other subjects and the degree of symptoms will be less exaggerated, not substantially affecting the person's ability to function.

Bipolar mood swings don't usually make sense. Even the person who is having them may not know why he or she is feeling so good or so bad. Bipolar mood swings are regulated by chemicals in the brain that are not responding appropriately.

There are some drugs that can simulate bipolar episodes, in fact, because the disorder is believed to be almost totally chemical, it is possible that ingesting certain chemicals can create an episode that is nearly identical to the bipolar one. It is also possible that ingesting chemicals could unbalance the brain to the point that it will not recover, so that bipolar symptoms becomes permanent and may require medication from that point on to control.

Whether drugs cause bipolar disorder or merely trigger an episode in a person who is prone to bipolar is really a discussion for scientists and not particularly important to this discussion. I do try to impress upon our children that though they may not have any symptoms now, they don't know for sure that they aren't predisposed to this disorder and they need to make sure they don't accidentally trigger an episode with alcohol or other recreational drugs. Of course, they don't actually listen, but I try.

Sleep deprivation can also cause symptoms of both mania and depression in different people at different times.

Just as there are many causes for seizures and they must be ruled out before a diagnosis of epilepsy is made, so the other possible causes of manic and depressive symptoms must be ruled out before a diagnosis of bipolar disorder is made.

Now that we understand what the symptoms of bipolar are, we can move on to that discussion of which behaviors are bipolar, which are from other mental illness, and which are merely a part of the personality. If you want to use this information to decide how much you should hold a person responsible for and how much you should forgive, you have a more difficult problem than you might believe.

A person is morally responsible for all behavior whether stable and rational at the time or not. You are no less injured when you are hit or yelled at or called names by a person who has psychotic mania than you are by the average healthy jerk. If you give a person freedom to behave badly without consequences when they are "in episode," they have less motivation to get treatment even if they become rational enough to be considering it. If episodes have consequences—especially really hard consequences--wouldn't that make it a little more worthwhile to avoid them?

Being in an episode makes it harder to act rationally, and there are times when a false belief causes someone to do the wrong thing for the right reason. But they can always control their behavior in some way and making them responsible to do that is perfectly rational and acceptable. You may be more inclined to forgive an action that was based on a false belief—when the person did what would have been the right thing if the situation were what it seemed at that time. But it does not mean that the person shouldn't be required to correct any problems created.

Let me make this more concrete. As an example: A man wakes up in the middle of the night, hears a strange noise and pushes his wife and two children out a second story window, causing minor injuries to all, including a few broken bones. Does he deserve to be locked up? Should his wife leave and never come back?

What if the sound he heard was a fire and he has saved them all from burning in their sleep or a burglar with a gun who has already killed another family down the street?

Ok, now what if that noise was entirely in his head or what if he had misinterpreted a real noise? What if there was no real danger, but there was a terrible danger in his mind? Is he still guilty? Motivation does count, even if you are equally injured either way, and understanding it is a lot more complicated than answering "was he sane when he did it?"

Don't automatically forgive an offense that is committed during an episode, or say that you'd never forgive a certain behavior and judge others for tolerating it. You never really know another person's mind and motivation. And you don't know what you would tolerate until you've been through it.

One good reason for learning what behaviors are symptoms of bipolar disorder and what behaviors might have other causes is to know when to get help and what kind of help to get. It is a good idea to watch for behaviors that aren't necessarily standard symptoms, but are signs that your partner is "ramping up," getting a bit too hyper, becoming manic.

One sign I notice is Troy getting very affectionate in a "fourth grader in love" sort of way. Another is cleaning—Troy doesn't do housework unless he's getting manic or I'm pushing him to help around the house. But when he's manic, he will wash a sink load of dishes or pick up a room without being asked.

For me, the ramping up behavior can be rather pleasant, but knowing where it is going makes me want to step right up and put a stop to it. I love having the housework done when I get home from work, but not if it means I'll be dealing with a raging monster by bedtime.

Knowing the signs can help you to be prepared and if you can arrange that your partner has a medication that can be added or increased in case of mania, you can sometimes nip it in the bud and avoid a full-blown episode. Remember, anything can trigger a mood swing, but the surest way to stop one is with medication. There are other things you can do if you don't have access to appropriate medications, but they are usually harder to pull off and have a greater risk of failure.

What can you do if medication is not available and your partner is ramping up? Remain calm. Speak quietly and slowly. Avoid arguments even if you have to agree to something you know is ridiculous. It may be best to agree to "look into it" or "discuss it later" if it's likely to blow up in your face otherwise. If there is any memory later, you should be able to talk your way out of it when your spouse is rational. (The memory loss that often comes with an episode can come in handy here.)

Plan an impromptu Thanksgiving dinner (I know tryptophan won't work miracles, but it can't hurt) or use comfort foods like macaroni and cheese. Keep a stash of decaf coffer on hand for this type of occasion. Serve chamomile tea or hot cocoa. Suggest activities that run off excess energy harmlessly. As a last resort before heading to the emergency room, separate yourself and get some breathing space to think out your strategy.

What can you do if medication is not an option and your partner is spiraling down? Remain calm. Speak quietly and slowly. Avoid arguments even if you have to agree to something you know is ridiculous.

Serve comfort foods. Try to engage the person in some sort of physical activity—exercise is a natural anti-depressant. Be aware of what is playing on the radio—some songs contribute to suicidal or homicidal ideation. Keep the atmosphere upbeat or calming.

Listen for signs of suicidal ideation and get immediate help from an emergency room or suicide helpline if you notice anything that worries you. Never ignore suicidal ideas—mistakes here can be fatal.

List the symptoms you've come to recognize in your partner as manic symptoms:

Is there some behavior or symptom that signals to you that things are heading in a bad direction? What are some signs of "ramping up" or becoming manic?

List some symptoms that you recognize as depression in your partner, be specific:

Is there some behavior or symptom that signals to you that things are heading in a bad direction? What are the signs that your partner is spiraling into depression?'

What strategies have you used successfully to lessen an episode or nip it in the bud?

What new strategies are you considering trying?

Symptom Review

There are many symptoms of bipolar and how they present can vary from person to person. Although the disorder might cause a person to believe things that are not true, people still have a free will and are responsible for their actions. If you know how the symptoms look in your partner, you can help to avoid or improve episodes.

In general, if you feel like your partner is in slow motion, that's depression. If you sense that things are on "fast forward," that's mania. Most depressed people are visibly unhappy, but not always—it is a rare mania that is marked by the euphoria that we were taught to expect.

We have to speak about this in general terms here, but you should know that these are just generalities and that what you experience could be totally different and still within the limits of what is common to bipolar disorder. Gathering information from many sources, including doctors, support groups, the Internet and the library is better than anything one book can provide.

The Bipolar Parent

Having a parent with bipolar disorder will affect any child in some way. If you can't make that a positive thing, can you protect them from the chaos?

When my husband was abusive and undiagnosed, I tried to protect my sons from the violence and chaos and I think I was about as successful as I could have been under the circumstance. Although I managed to keep them safe from their father's attacks, I do think that they all have some level of post-traumatic stress disorder from having grown up with an unstable father in the house.

The controversy rages on over which is more damaging—the divorce and the problems that come with it or living with an unstable and often irrational parent. I really don't think there is one answer to that, and I suspect that choices have to be made based on a lot of individual circumstances. If it's making you, as an adult, nervous to be at home, it's probably not a good environment to raise children. But even if you are coping alright, it doesn't naturally follow that children will have all of the skills needed to live healthy or happy lives.

Be aware that if your partner is also the biological parent of your children, you may be required to share custody and the court could require you to allow your unstable ex- to spend time with your children without supervision. If that person might abuse or neglect the children, make sure you have ample evidence of this before you go to court or divorce could be the worst thing for the children. You want to get them away from the chaos, not leave them alone in the center of it.

One thing that I think has been helpful for my sons is something we call a reality check. There are times when their father behaves in ways that are totally irrational and unpredictable. Sometimes you hear the delusions so often that you start to wonder, "who is the sane one here anyway?"

We have a sort of family code that goes something like this: "Reality check. Did Dad really say that he wants me to go outside and fight him? Is he for real?" "Yes, he really said that, but he's not being rational so you might want to go to a friend's house for a while until he is calmer."

It is a tough balancing act for children to respect a mentally ill parent. If they do as they are told in the same way that they would with a healthy parent, they might get into some serious trouble. Rather than expecting children to know a "lawful order" when they hear one, suggest that they double check with the other parent if there is any doubt.

It also works to protect your sanity if you can double check to make sure you just heard what you know you just heard. I know there have been times when I have questioned my sanity in the middle of an episode because I was hearing things that I just couldn't imagine my husband actually saying—but there it was, coming straight out of his mouth. As the boys grew older, they were able to help me sort out what was real with the same type of reality check, often before I even asked for it.

My sons have an unusual number of adult friends—at church, at school, and in the community. I believe that they have sought out other adults, as healthy role models, as strong parental figures, and just to have someone to talk with who is outside their peer group and less likely to judge them or gossip about them.

I have also supplemented this by offering them all the opportunity to meet with their own therapist—we even took the whole gang to meet together and separately with their father's therapist to discuss the possibility of individual therapy. There are several therapists at the clinic that could be filled in on the home situation and none of them would break confidentiality with the children.

Only our youngest decided to go that route, but it was a choice that each of them had to make. If you have younger children (our youngest was 12 at the time of diagnosis) you may want to make that decision for them and set them up with a therapist on a trial basis to see if it is helpful.

A therapist can help a child learn coping skills. Not only are there new stresses to cope with when you have a bipolar parent, but you may also have an excellent example of what NOT to do. If the child sees a parent with bipolar disorder behaving in ways that are not appropriate, they can learn those behaviors instead of more useful behaviors.

A child might find it hard to grow out of the "temper tantrum" stage if they see a parent using tantrums to control other people. Learning to share, learning to disagree constructively, learning to have rational discussions, are all harder in a home where both parents do not consistently demonstrate those skills. Without a therapist, you will have to make a point of teaching these things and un-teaching any other troubling behavior that you notice.

Do be careful of who knows that your child is seeing a therapist. There is still a world of stigma out there and a child can be tortured at school if the wrong person learns that he or she is seeing a therapist, regardless of the reason. I don't see this as a family secret, more a privacy issue, but it is important that your child has that privacy. We don't want to raise our children believing that mental illness or seeing a therapist is a secret—that only feeds the stigma—but allowing other children to know too much could lead to unnecessary trouble.

Give your child the appropriate information to share with classmates and teachers about your spouse's condition. If your spouse is ever in episode at a school event, it's going to be pretty hard to keep the condition a secret, but it is usually fairly easy to hide for short periods.

If your child is likely to describe behavior and incidents, you may want to be prepared to explain things to teachers, social workers, and the police. While you might not want the child discussing the diagnosis, stories that include the idea that a doctor is involved might be less problematic.

We have been pretty open about it and had no major problems, so far. Then again, my children were all teenagers when their father was diagnosed.

You may find yourself speaking with child protection case workers at some time. Your child may mention something that worries a doctor or teacher or act out in ways that draw attention. It is best to be as calm and as truthful as possible. You may find yourself educating these people about mental illness, though most of them do come across it often in their work.

We had a case of father and son both in an irritable, hypo-manic mood at the same time before school one morning. Fireworks! A caseworker met me at work and asked me to stop by his office as soon as possible.

I told the caseworker that I really didn't know if what had happened constituted abuse because I had already left for work at the time, but that we did recognize the mental illness and were treating it with the help of a psychiatrist at the local mental health clinic.

I explained that we had set up some safety nets; our son was permitted to go to his brother's apartment if he felt uncomfortable with his father at any time, he could call me on his cell phone, and he had other adult friends he could contact.

While we agreed that the situation is not ideal, the case worker admitted that we had done everything he could think of and that our son was probably as safe as most children in "normal" families. No case was opened.

Make sure that your spouse has a back-up plan for child care when symptoms start while you are away. If the child is very young, a close family member who agrees to be available might be a good choice. An older child might simply go to a friend's house to play when asked or when they see symptoms that make them uncomfortable. You will need to have an agreement in place that your spouse will not track the child down and punish him for leaving—even if the child sometimes takes advantage of this plan unnecessarily.

You may not want to think about it, but it is entirely possible that your child will inherit the genetic material for bipolar disorder or other mood disorders. There are statistics available, but you will not really know unless the disorder shows itself. You can deal with a bipolar child and a bipolar spouse with the methods you are learning, but it is definitely not for the fainthearted. It will draw you closer to God or your support group.

Your child may also develop personality disorders or post-traumatic stress disorder. These disorders are caused by the chaos that is often present with an unstable parent, which is one reason prompt and successful treatment is so important when there are children at home.

Therapy to learn appropriate coping techniques can help a child avoid learning the ones that lead to personality disorders. If you see any signs that the child is nervous, unhappy, angry or "not himself" for more than a few days, please arrange for some sort of professional intervention. In most places there is free access to mental health care for children either through the medical system or the public schools. No excuses.

I honestly believe that if you do the best you can, take whatever help is offered and avoid being defensive about your parenting skills you can raise healthy children. Every family has issues—you have the advantage of knowing that mental illness is one of yours. Reread the boundaries section and set up boundaries for your children if you haven't already.

Boundaries for Children

Make a list of the boundaries that you need to protect your children and plan can be done to protect those boundaries.

My children want/need	I will
Ex: Physical Safety	Remove them from the home when I sense danger

Make a list of boundaries that your children will be required to respect.

I need	I will
Peace in the house	Send everyone to their respective room when a disagreement cannot be solved peacefully

The World of Work

There's something out there for everyone, except...

Many people with bipolar disorder do work regular jobs. Some work seems custom-made for people with bipolar disorder—creative or artistic work that can be done in short bursts of energy. Private practice doctors and lawyers may be able to schedule their work around their mood swings as long as there are few extended periods of depression. Consultants, realtors and even sales people may get enough accomplished during hypomanic periods to ride out the less productive parts of the cycle.

At some point, your spouse may discover that the jobs have run out and the career choices are getting lost to sick days and manic tirades. When this happens you will have to figure out ways to support your family with one person (you) working as both the breadwinner and the homemaker without the perk of being free to make major decisions alone as you would if you were single.

It is best to face this calmly and with a sense of humor, so this list of reasons a person with bipolar might have trouble working a regular job should come in handy.

Why Can't an Intelligent Creative Person With Bipolar Disorder Hold a Job?

- Because the work is too stressful and leads to depression.
- Because the work is too exciting and leads to mania.
- Because the boss is an idiot and doesn't know what he's doing.
- Because everyone there is just plain stupid.
- Because the work is SO beneath me.
- Because the hours are too long.
- Because the hours are too short.

- Because the hours are too early.
- Because the hours are too late.
- Because I can go in whenever I want, but I never want.
- Because life is too short.
- Because it doesn't pay enough.
- Because it isn't meaningful.
- Because work isn't fun.
- Because the other workers aren't taking it seriously.
- Because everyone is too serious.
- Because another employee was looking at me funny.
- Because another employee was looking at my spouse.
- Because I don't feel like it.
- Because the whole material thing is just too…
- Because they are all out to get me.
- Because they know I know more than they do and they are afraid I'll take their job.
- Because I'm overqualified.
- Because it's not in my field.
- Because I'm too depressed.
- Because I'm too tired.
- Because I have better things to do.
- Because I'm too good for that.
- Because I made a perfectly good suggestion and the boss didn't do it.
- Because the boss is a jerk and I said so.
- Because it's Monday.
- Are you kidding?

(You're right, that's not really funny—except it is so true.)

I didn't know that I would be financially supporting my family alone, and you probably won't either. It may happen that one serious episode ends the chances for employment indefinitely, but more likely, it will just sneak up on you like it did on us.

It starts with a string of jobs that don't seem to be lasting very long. You may even see it as a positive thing—if the jobs seem to keep getting better or the pay higher—so as long as your spouse is working regularly, it's not a problem.

Then you start to notice a lot of time lapsing between jobs and even if you have been doing great on your part, the bills start backing up. You hate to bring it up to someone who is already miserable about not being able to find an appropriate job. But the pressure can get to you and arguments about money, about sharing the work around the house, about who you are and how you relate to one another, just come out of nowhere and never seem to stop.

It may be time to consider applying for Social Security Disability. This can be tricky business because this disorder is sneaky. You know that your partner, who may be perfectly employable and a great asset to any organization nine days out of ten, is totally unemployable and a menace to society just often enough to make wise employers run for the hills.

How can someone who looks so good in an interview, at the psychiatrist's office, at church, in front of friends and family, be so invisibly disabled. And still, they are. If a person is not employable on regular working days during regular working hours more often than not, that person is, by definition, disabled. Too bad you can't put a cast on the brain or take a blood test or something that would make this more real to the world, but it is totally and entirely real—and we both know it.

Social Security Disability may be the safety net that you need to keep the house, the car, and the power bills paid. In some cases, all you have to do is fill out all of the appropriate paperwork, get the doctor to fill out paperwork (this is where we had problems) and wait. In many cases, you will need to hire an attorney (find one who knows the system and understands mental illness) and gather information for a hearing. Either way, it doesn't hurt to try. The worst that can happen is that you don't get anything—you definitely won't if you don't try.

There are also insurance plans that pay out when a person is totally and permanently disabled. If there is one of these in place, you need to read the fine print and find out whether you can file a claim for mental illness or not. Some are very specific about what type of disability is covered, while others are much more general. Find out what you're up against.

It is possible that you will have to do everything yourself without financial aid from any disability insurance. If this is the case, go back and read the first section of this book again because you really do need to take good care of yourself to maintain your own health and sanity. It is hard work but you can do it. You are probably already doing it and somehow you are surviving. It helps NOT to think about this being permanent—better to concentrate on the problems directly in front of you today and not worry too much about the abstract troubles of the future.

Anything can happen. This might not be permanent. The right combination of meds over the right period of time, discovering a talent or career field that works with the bipolar cycles, winning the lottery (Now, don't go telling me that this is your best shot—it only seems that way.) or even the right training could put you back on track. Then there's the possibility of divorce and remarriage to a healthy partner. Anything can happen.

Employment Plan

The first thing you need to do is to determine whether or not your partner is capable of permanent full-time employment or if that is even what you both want. There are many single-income families making ends meet. Start with a budget chart. When you compare the value of a second income, remember that there are expenses related to working that often make that second income less desirable. It's usually best to work on a one month chart.

Item	Income	Expense	Total
My Job	$		
Rent		$	
Power		$	
Phone		$	
Water/sewer		$	
Food/household		$	
Entertainment		$	
Car (+gas, oil)		$	
Other income less expenses	$	$	$
Total			$

If one income doesn't cover the basic expenses, it may be possible to scale back on some expenses. One purpose of a budget is to see where you are overspending. There are ideas on the getolife.org website for saving money that will be available in a book form soon.

While collecting on disability insurance or social security disability might seem a natural choice, remember that it is not a quick fix. It may take months or even years to get approved for disability income. You need some way to make ends meet while you are waiting.

If you can't reduce expenses you will need to find some way to add income. This could be finding a job that is appropriate for your bipolar spouse or it could mean keeping an open mind to other options.

Have you considered a hobby that might provide a source of income? Many craft items can be sold through consignment shops. Hobbies can be shared through teaching a class at a local library or community college. A person with bipolar disorder might easily be able to get through an hour or two of sharing a hobby once or twice a week, even if working full-time is impossible.

Have you considered finding a better paying job for yourself? This seems to be the most intimidating idea, but there are many people who are underemployed because they need the flexible schedule that lower paying jobs provide. If you look closely, though, you might find that higher paying jobs with flexible schedules are also out there. It certainly doesn't hurt to look. You don't have to quit your day job.

While a person with bipolar disorder has some serious limitations, it is more than a useful exercise for your spouse to make a list of his or her skills and abilities. Do not look for ways to connect those to a job description until you can't think of anything more to add to your list. There's a whole book out there of uses for a dead cat: if you can't list more uses for yourself, you're in trouble. Expect to spend more than one session on this. If it doesn't lead to a few ideas to earn money, it should at least help you to find a few constructive things to do with yourself.

Come back after a day or two and see if you see any new possibilities. Look at the list together with your partner—two heads may be better than one.

I wish I could tell you that you won't fall into the gap between legally disabled and actually employable, but it's a big gap and people fall through. You will both survive. It will be scary and hard and it won't help the stress level a bit, but you will survive.

Take a deep breath. Repeat.

Where Do I Go From Here?

Chapter 12

You may be able to deal with the disorder
with the help of appropriate professionals,
but perhaps you feel the need to protect
your children from the chaos or maybe
there are problems with getting treatment.
Maybe you just can't take it anymore.
What can you do?

Things sometimes get to a point where you just want to give up and run away. But as a stable adult, particularly if there are children in the picture, you have to make plans, work out all of the possibilities, and protect yourself and your children. Duck and run just won't cut it.

I am not a lawyer and even if I were, I could not speak for all situations in all locations because the laws are different. In areas where laws are similar, they still play out differently. Even if you are not seriously considering bankruptcy, divorce or legal separation, it may be in your best interest to visit an attorney and ask a few questions about your rights and responsibilities.

If you are considering a divorce, find out how things are likely to play out in court with regards to child custody issues. Although you may be hoping to help your child escape the chaos of living with someone with serious mental illness, you could actually make matters worse by being forced to allow the parent with bipolar disorder to demand parental rights even when in episode and unable to take on parental responsibilities. The courts are supposed to protect the rights of children to be safe and comfortable, but there are some pretty frightening possibilities.

Be especially careful if you are a man—I know of women with serious cases of bipolar who have been able to pull it together long enough to convince a judge that they should have physical custody. Some even bring paranoid delusions to court and are able to convince authorities that they are innocent victims and that the husbands are the dangerous ones. How can you protect your child from someone who has physical custody when you only see your child on weekends?

That doesn't mean you should stay in an abusive relationship, but it does mean that you should gather as much real evidence as possible of the damage that comes from bipolar behavior. If there is violence, take photos. If there are threatening emails, print out copies and also save them to a file. Let phone calls go to an answering machine and save the recorded messages. If possible, record rages on audio or video tape. Find out who has seen this side of your spouse and ask if they would be willing to provide witness testimony. Even if criminal charges are never brought, this evidence can be used by your divorce lawyer. You may be able to protect yourself and your children without this, but it is worth the trouble to get the cards stacked in your favor.

I have seen the children of bipolar single mothers and it's not an easy situation for them. They end up with a lot of co-dependent behaviors that do not serve them well in the real world. Children who are required to care for an unstable parent do not get anything like a normal childhood and this can be hazardous to their health.

If you are the stable parent, please, do everything within your power to maintain contact, to retain or share custody, and to make sure that when the other parent is not stable, the children are safe.

If you are considering leaving the relationship for financial reasons, even if that is only one of many reasons, make sure that you explain that to your attorney. There may be specific steps that need to be taken to separate your debts and assets before going to court. It is possible that you will need to file for bankruptcy at the time of the divorce in order to avoid taking on all of your partner's debt.

There may also be ways of protecting your financial situation without actually going through a divorce. It really depends on your situation, on the laws in your area and on how those laws will be interpreted in your case.

Only an attorney who is licensed to practice in your location will be able to sort that out for you. If you are worried about losing your home because your partner is spending the mortgage money on EBay, call an attorney and find out what your options are. You may be surprised at the options that are available to you, but you won't know until you ask.

Yes, attorneys are expensive, but usually you can get an initial consultation for a fixed fee or even free. There are legal aid attorneys for those with little or no income, and the price could quickly be recovered if you end up in divorce or bankruptcy court.

Maybe you've gone through financial ruins, physical attacks and cheating, but after a diagnosis and starting medication, you feel that your marriage has a chance and you want to put it back together again.

I won't tell you that it's going to be easy, but if your spouse is willing to stick with the program, it isn't impossible either. Build a relationship with your partner's doctors—you are an important part of the treatment team. Establish boundaries that keep you comfortable and safe in your marriage. Know what you want and what you can expect in your relationship. Do what it takes to make YOU happy.

It may take some time and effort to regain the intimacy you want in your marriage. Sometimes it feels like you are sleeping with a child when your spouse has been behaving like a child and sometimes you are just plain exhausted and don't have the energy to deal with it.

It is alright to say "no" to sexual activity when your spouse is hypersexual and you are not interested for any reason, but it is also alright to say "yes" to sex even if you haven't really been feeling intimate.

You may have to use your imagination to remember that the person that you married is still inside that body, especially if he or she is rarely discernable. Remind yourself that this really is your partner and that it is not wrong to engage in sexual activity, even hypersexual activity, with your spouse.

You have to do what makes you feel comfortable. You are not forcing your spouse to cheat if you are not available for sex at any moment. It is a choice. It is great if you can agree on these things, but even in the best of marriages, there will be differences.

Life isn't about winning or losing. Success isn't about fame or money. Success is that you actually do what is important to you, that you are comfortable with who you are and what you are doing. The secret of life isn't to have all the toys, it's to share what you have and be content. There are worse things in the world than having a partner with a serious mental illness, even if I can't think of one at the moment.

Decision Book

Too Good to Leave, Too Bad to Stay by Mira Kirshenbaum is a diagnostic flowchart for relationships. Answer a list of questions to determine whether the relationship is likely to be salvageable. Her recommendations are based on statistics from people who have stayed or left similar relationships. If you can't make up your mind, or if you know what you want, but need a good reason, this book will help you sort things out.

End Notes

There's always something more.

As I was trying to do the final edits, I kept stumbling on things that I had written on the topic that I really should have put into the book somehow, but hadn't. I had friends and people I barely knew telling me to "just finish the book already, there are people who need to read it." So instead of doing another rewrite, as tempting as that has been, I decided to add a couple chapters as a sort of Post Script.

I want you to know that this book is not the final word on how to survive a marriage with someone who has bipolar. I've read a lot of good advice in self-help books, and a lot of books that really just don't apply to the situations we find ourselves in.

I personally like Dobson, Cloud and Townsend, and a few others, but I do get frustrated when advice is given like it's a direct command from God but it obviously doesn't apply in my life situation. What I find interesting is that some books fall flat when you don't have the perfect healthy situation, while others seem to apply to a much broader range of situations without even really trying.

Dobson's books on raising children don't fall apart when you have a bipolar child or even when you are raising that child with a bipolar spouse. And we all know that the Cloud and Townsend books on relationships don't lose anything when your situation isn't "normal".

You shouldn't feel guilty or wrong or whatever about doing the opposite of what normal authorities say—they are written from a very narrow human perspective—and the advice does not apply to your situation. If you did all of the right things according to those experts you might get yourself killed.

It's like putting everyone on the same healthy diet whether they are diabetic or allergic to nuts or suffering from a vitamin deficiency, whether they are a 50 pound child or a 250 pound man. Sure, there are general rules for what makes a healthy diet, but those rules apply differently in different situations.

People who offer advice in a "one size fits all" authoritarian way are wrong. It's taken me a long time to figure that out—so I hope that by mentioning it here I can save someone the aggravation. All advice in this book is intended as one idea of how this can work—I share my experience so that you can avoid my mistakes and copy my successes, but your results, like your family, will vary.

The following are items that were added at the last possible minute that didn't fit neatly into the foregoing chapters. There are some personal stories that give you a brief glimpse into my life as I see it. There are other perspectives and I'm sure my sons would tell these stories differently, but these stories authenticate that I'm not an expert in the book-learning sense. I'm just one person who has been there and done that without being destroyed in the process. Our sons are real normal people—sometimes they go a little crazy under the pressure, but they are basically good people learning to thrive in less than ideal circumstances. I considered changing names to protect the boys, but those who know them will know them and those who don't know them, won't care.

Some of the humor in that last chapter is a bit politically incorrect, but there are days when if you don't learn to laugh, you're doomed to cry.

Our House

Chapter 13

Sometimes miracles happen—this one happened to me.

Just after Troy (my husband) had been diagnosed, and before he was approved for disability, we started thinking about buying a house because the apartment we were renting had been foreclosed on by the bank. Our landlord just disappeared and no one was making repairs so we were heating with kerosene and buying water by the gallon jug because the water pipes burst in the cold after the furnace died. In February. In Illinois. I think the place might have been condemned if the inspector were brave enough to enter—even the rats and roaches were looking for better digs. <DOWN>

We had arranged financing and were given a range of how much money the mortgage company would approve us for, so we looked around, hoping to find something we liked and that was in our price range. <UP>

We found a house that was absolutely perfect. We looked at other houses and a few were nicer, but this house had everything that was important to us and a few things we didn't even know we were looking for. I could feel something when I walked in for the first time-the place was a mess, it hadn't been cleaned since the previous tenants moved out and left a lot of stuff, but it felt good to be in that house. <UP>

There was a fenced in back yard—with an area that was fenced in separately from the main yard where the dogs could run and a concrete slab in the back for a garage or an above-ground pool. <UP>

We went through a lot of ups and downs trying to get the house. At first it was priced too low and the bank had a lien on it for more than the owner was asking-so we weren't even given an answer to our offer for four weeks. <DOWN>

Most of the places needed a lot of work and none were even close to that first house. We finally got an answer from the bank-they would need more money, nearly twice what was originally asked, but we could do that-the mortgage company would cover it and we could come up with the money for the down payment. We put in another offer. The offer was accepted. <UP>

We had a closing date on Monday and everything was going great until we got a call on Thursday night that the appraisal had come in lower than the agreed price. The mortgage company wouldn't loan us the money. <DOWN>

On Friday our realtor called and said that the bank that owned the property wanted us to apply to their mortgage department to see if we could qualify through them. Troy (my dh and bpso) walked to the bank (our car was acting up) and got the paperwork filled out. <UP>

Our credit is far from perfect. We had credit cards when Troy lost his last job 10 years ago that never did get paid. I have just got my student loan back on track and we have very little current debt. We really didn't think we had a chance with a regular bank. We were going through a mortgage company that specializes in high risk, high interest loans. Troy brought me the paperwork to sign. No promises, but it's worth a shot. <Terror>

The bank's board met on Friday afternoon and the bank really wanted to get that property dealt with-or, as I prefer to believe, God was sitting in with the board and making suggestions. We got the mortgage. Not a special high interest loan-a regular 30 year mortgage. We even qualify for a $5000 grant to help with the down payment, so we can use some of the money we had saved for that to buy another car. Our payments (even with insurance and property taxes) will be very close to what we have been paying to rent a dump. <UP>

I've been playing with the math-what we could save if we pay every payday, etc. And I realized something. If we had got the property at the original lower price, but with the higher interest loan, we'd probably end up paying as much or more in the long run and we'd be paying an out of town mortgage company. Now we can drop off our payments at a local bank (or transfer the money from my account) and talk to a real person if we have questions or problems. We close on Wednesday instead of Monday, so we have to wait two more days, but we have the house.

Troy was still a bit manic from the whole experience and if he maintains a bit of that through the move, we will be in good shape. I do worry that he will sink into depression and leave me to move alone, but I have teenaged sons who are excited about moving and willing to help, so I'm not terribly worried-we'll manage one way or another. If we spend the first night in the house and everything is wonderful, he may be manic enough to move everything before I get home from work on Thursday (you know how productive a good manic episode can be).

Our youth leader loaned us his truck to move. Here's another act of God-his wife used to work in another city about 20 miles away, but because she started working just a couple blocks from home, they can share her car to get to work and he won't need the truck so we can have it for a few days to get everything moved without it being much of a problem for them.

Troy crashed after the first day of moving. We got the appliances and big things, and most of the boxes I'd packed, but it would be months before we realized exactly how much we had abandoned at the apartment. We can replace most of the stuff and I've dealt with worse than a few missing mementos. <DOWN>

This whole experience has almost made me understand what it must feel like to be bipolar-the ups and downs have been rational, but incredibly frustrating, too. I really believed everything would work itself out in the end, but there were times when I just couldn't see how.

We have gone through some ups and downs in the new house. It's 125 years old, but it's new to us. We had some water leaks at first, but plumbing is fairly straightforward to repair. It appears that the electrical service was installed piecemeal as it was needed—so it may need to be changed at some point in the future, but...

The yard is wonderful. Morning glories grow over the fence that divides the dog yard from the rest of the yard and hummingbirds come to sip from the morning glories. We added hummingbird feeders after we noticed the birds in the yard and now we see them all summer.

We also added a regular bird feeder. Last year we had a nest of robins in a tree just outside our bedroom window. This year we had a cardinals' nest on the "dog fence" right outside the door to the porch.

We are remodeling the kitchen and downstairs bath. There was a toilet right in front of a sliding glass door that just felt "wrong" and we found that there was a place where a toilet had been removed around the corner—so we moved it back. Other than that, we are just making it our own.

Whenever I think that my life is terrible and that nobody cares, I try to remember that things were once a whole lot worse and that I received a miracle.

My Bad Week

Any time you think you've got things figured out—WHAM !

This little story happened toward the end of writing this book, when Troy had been stable for a while and things were going along pretty smoothly. I'm including it to show that episodes can happen at any time and that it is possible to deal with them with humor and patience.

If you had the naïve idea that once you have a diagnosis and full compliance with therapy that everything will fall into place and you will be able to live happily ever after, I'm sorry to burst your bubble.

While I have no intention of ever leaving my marriage and know that we are about as happy as any other married couple, we do have our moments and I want to tell you about one of them.

 I knew it would be an interesting day because Troy (my bipolar husband) had been complaining about suicidal thoughts and was contemplating the hospital. I asked him to make me a dental appointment, because I had a toothache and with 10 hour days and no phone that dials out, it would be easier for him-so I knew he would call and let me know when the appointment was made.

My 18 year old son, TJ, mentioned that his younger brother had been texting him that he didn't feel well and asking him to pick him up from school—he gets there about an hour before I leave for work and already he's complaining before I leave for work. Yeah, just your average day.

So I start getting phone calls about an hour after I get to work-Troy, telling me that he's going to leave the phone at home if he goes to the emergency room and will take the truck if he finds the keys so I can have the car if they keep him. He's still not sure he wants to go.

Maybe twenty minutes later-Josh (youngest son) whining that his stomach is turning and he's getting a headache and he can't concentrate anyways.

I talk to the school nurse and she tells me that he already has too many absences and he will need a doctor's excuse to miss another day of school. Since I know that he is not contagious and that what he is describing is exactly what he's had in the past, I suggest that he try to tough it out, rest in the nurse's office and at least get his homework for his classes and do what he can. He's not exactly happy, but he'll try.

About an hour after that--TJ (older son) calls to ask if he needs to go pick up his brother. I tell him that he's trying to get through the rest of the day and will text if he needs to come home. It occurs to me that "home" is not exactly the best place to be since there is already one depressed person there, but.

Troy calls just before lunch. He couldn't get a dental appointment on one of my days off, but I have one at 7:30 in the morning on the one weekday next week before I work the full ten hours. Not exactly what I was hoping, but you don't turn down a dental appointment when you have a tooth ache. Fine.

Shortly after lunch Josh calls back, he's not getting better and he really wants to go home. I talk to the nurse and tell her that if he can't be productive at school, he may as well have his brother pick him up.

By the time I get home at 7:30pm, Josh is helping Chris (older brother) polish Chris' car. I ask what he's going to do about missing school. He tells me that it was almost the end of the day anyways, so he didn't call for a ride. Fine.

I come inside, half expecting to see the phone in Troy's chair, but there he is. He tells me that he did get up and out today. He took Josh to mow a lawn for a lady from church, and then he took Josh to softball practice. He's a busy kid for being so sick. Troy still feels depressed and miserable, but doesn't want to go to the hospital because he doesn't think there is much they can do for him.

Suicidal thoughts DO worry me, but his thoughts are not well-formed and he is the one who suggested the hospital, so I know he doesn't want to follow through on them, so he can spend another day in his chair. I don't think dynamite would move him.

I didn't do much of anything today besides working my usual ten hour shift as a cosmetics clerk at Walgreen Drug, but I feel tired. I can't imagine why. I'm glad the next day is my day off.

I spent the whole next afternoon-from about 11:30 to almost 6 sitting in the hospital waiting for them to admit Troy because his suicidal thoughts are bothering him. When he finally gets to the part where he signs the paperwork, he tries to back out. They told him that he would have to convince the doctor that he was alright or he would be involuntarily admitted. So he went along peacefully.

I had signed up for a class at the library at 6:00 (medicinal herbs) and Troy told me that I should go ahead and go, that I could miss the 6-7pm visiting hours since we had spent my whole day off at the hospital and I needed the break. He did want me to get some clothes together (he didn't think about that before he went in?) and bring them to him-nothing with strings or anything dangerous-but clean socks and underwear, some jeans and T-shirts. I'd already washed some things and put in another load before leaving for the class. Told the kids I'd be out for an hour or two and to start dinner without me if they got hungry.

I went to the class on my scooter (I think I am now known as the crazy scooter lady because I drive the thing in all weather unless it's pouring rain when I leave for work-can't work in wet clothes).

The speaker has a bit of laryngitis, so she's talking in whispers and about quarter to seven my phone rings-I run out of the room to answer it-it's Chris, my 21 year old son, wondering if I need a ride home. I'm going to be here at least a while longer, so tell him I'll call if the weather is bad when I want to come home. I'm fine.

I get back to my seat and they are passing around samples of herbs, dried herbs, tinctures, teas, etc. to show how herbs are preserved and used. She's talking about the things you can do to stay healthy: like limiting stress-do I laugh or cry at this point?-and some recipes for "tonics" to clean out your digestive system and some antioxidants to boost immunity.

Another half hour and I get another phone call-rush out of the room-a cell phone is really loud when the class is being held at a whisper, even with the microphone. It's Troy wondering when we will be bringing his clothes. He's spent the afternoon in hospital clothes and wants real clothes. I explain that I'm in the class I was planning to go to and that I'd have his clothes in the morning.

I'm really interested in the class, but it's hard to focus. Good thing there are take-home notes. I'm sure the instructor thinks I'm crazy or rude or something, but I just had my husband admitted to the mental ward-it's not exactly a normal day. By the time the class ends, I am noticing that the rain is slowing down and I'm hoping that I can get home on my scooter. I go through some frantic searching for the keys-last time I lost the keys, the scooter disappeared. Deep breaths.

Found the keys, got home, the washer didn't do quite the spin cycle it is supposed to do and Troy's jeans are dripping, but I wring them a bit in my hands and toss them into the dryer.

Josh, 16, has found a "salamander" at the park and wants to go to the pet store for food. It's after 8 and the pet store might be closing, besides we have no idea what this thing eats. Pack it up, take it along, see if the pet store people can guess. The only person at the pet store is a kid Josh's age-I'm sure there's a manager somewhere, but nowhere in sight. We buy a bag of tiny crickets and cross our fingers.

The "salamander" turns out to be a skink-after considerable internet research-whole different category, from amphibian to reptile, but the same diet-there are a few positive things in my life still. He refuses to eat anything in front of us, but he should survive. Josh discovers that the bottom of our old tank is totaled, so he takes the thing to the neighbor's house where they have a big empty tank he can live in for now.

I'm tired so I start getting ready for bed. Realize that it's 11pm and Josh needs to get to bed-not an easy person to wake in the morning for school. He doesn't answer his phone and Chris' girlfriend offers to go get him from the neighbor's house.

He comes home in a huff-why do I have to be in bed so early (excuse me? Early? It's almost midnight!) and he slams the door. A few minutes later Chris goes into his room to ask how the skink is doing and discovers--no Josh. Now Chris is mad and screaming. He runs over to the neighbor's house.

Josh reappears in his other brother's downstairs bedroom with even more attitude than before. I'm too tired to deal with this-could everyone please just get to bed?

The alarm rings, I swear, the minute my head hits the pillow. It's time to get Josh up. He seems to be moving, but I have to keep at him or he'll fall back into bed. Never mind, there went the bus.

I drive Josh to school and when I'm just two blocks from home the car stalls at the corner. The gas gage is on empty. I knew that. Why didn't I just stop for gas? My mind is not in gear. I call home. No one answers. A man in a work van pulls up behind me and offers to push me off the road so I can go get help. See, another good thing.

I get home and TJ, my 18 year old son, is just getting up. He has a Jeep with a broken gas gage, so he has a 5 gallon gas can he can take and get gas for the car. Off to the gas station. $10 worth of gas and the thing starts right up. Yep, life is good.

Get home in time to realize that Troy's jeans still aren't quite dry and I have to get to work. Set the dryer heavy and ask TJ if he will drop the stuff off when the jeans get dry. I'm pretty sure they are worried that mom will crash and burn at any minute, so he agrees to get the stuff to his dad as soon as possible. It's pouring rain, so I take the car to work for the first time in months-at least I know it has gas.

Work was pretty quiet-an oasis-until a police officer shows up in my department and asks to talk to me about my son. What son? What happened to my son? Is this a conspiracy?

Josh is somehow involved with a cell phone being stolen at school. He didn't steal it and he only knows who did it based on the rumors at the school, but they need to talk to him and he refuses to talk without a parent. "OK, you can talk to him-but do not make him crazy. We've had a hard week."

An hour or so later I get a call from TJ. Josh has called the police and told the whole story, naming the person he believes took the phone. Josh is out of trouble with the police. Sigh.

I've had a terrible, horrible, no good, very bad day. Do you think there's room in Australia?

Keep it Light

Chapter 15

Sometimes life is too serious to take seriously. Find the humor in it.

Humor is a great stress reliever. Whether you throw a funny movie into the DVD player or read a good book, a little laughter relieves a lot of stress. Stress is a major trigger. You want to get rid of as many triggers as you can.

Living with a bipolar spouse can really take the fun out of things sometimes, but when you take the time to really think about it, there is still a lot of humor in our situation. These are some mood lighteners for use when your own mood starts to swing low.

1. What is the strangest thing the bipolar person in your life has bought while manic?

    The stuff no one else would buy on eBay is a popular answer

2. What is the strangest thing the bipolar person in your life has done while manic?

    They don't all run down the streets naked, but a lot of strange things do happen.

3. How close is the bipolar person in your life to beating the world record for hours without sleep while manic?

    This is a record invented specifically for mania.

4. How long can a person stay in bed while depressed?

    It only seems like forever.

5. What's the strangest argument you've ever had with a person with bipolar disorder?

> Persons in the middle of a mania will argue that the sky is green. And win.

6. What is good about someone with bipolar disorder?

> They can do almost anything while hypo-manic.

> They are easy to dust when depressed.

The answers to these questions are many and varied and they do help to keep us from taking ourselves and our problems too seriously. Caution, do not share any of this "humor" with a person who is in an irritable part of the cycle as this can be hazardous to your health and peace.

Our problems can be very serious. People suffering from bipolar can be very destructive and it is easy for the family to be caught in the crossfire. Whether it's overdrawing the checking account or throwing a tantrum in public, we're right there trying to make things right. But living day to day with some of those issues hanging over your head can be really overwhelming and looking at the funny side of things gives us an opportunity to laugh at ourselves and relax a bit so we can get a fresh perspective.

Pick a Card to Handle an Episode

I saw an ad for some pre-printed cards that have suggestions for defusing a person with bipolar when they go into an episode and thought: yeah, I'm going to suggest that he gets some exercise to relieve some stress-I could suggest sex after he's been chasing me around all afternoon and he'd get mad because I'm telling him what to do. (I'm so controlling.) I can't get my husband to go in the pool with me or to take a dog for a walk or anything when he's not "in the mood" for it. I'm pretty sure the cards being offered are intended for people who are serious about helping themselves--they are out there, just not in my house.

I decided to write a more realistic set of cards for my personal use:

1. Suggest that he yell at you and chase you around the house with a power-tool. (Great aerobic exercise.)

2. Suggest that he watch TV with his eyes shut and scream bloody murder when someone changes the channel. (Raises everyone's heart-rate at one time)

3. Suggest that he scream obscenities at the children that he can later punish them for repeating. (Get the whole family involved in an activity)

At least those are things he's likely to do.

Or maybe:

1. Suggest that he repeat that last comment because you don't think the hidden microphone got it. (That moment of silence when he lets that sink in is priceless)

2. Suggest that he lock the dog up before throwing a tantrum so they don't get in the way defending the children. (You don't want the dog getting in trouble over this.

3. Suggest that he count backwards from ten before he blasts off. It might stop him in his tracks or at least help you to detach. (Think NASA launch.)

Bipolar Quotes

What are your favorite "bipolar quotes," you know, the things you hear during an episode that would make you cry if you didn't have to laugh? Here are some of mine:

"If you really loved me..." If I never hear "If you really loved me..." one more time, I just might survive."If you really loved me you would understand what I want and do it even if it is totally irrational." The only correct response I can come up with is "If you loved me you wouldn't expect me to..." but that only works with rational people and when he's rational we don't get into this whole discussion.

Another favorite saying is "I'll try" which means: "I'll think about it, but it isn't likely to get beyond the thinking stage and if it actually happens, which is highly unlikely, even if it's something like getting out of bed or taking a shower, I expect a standing ovation and a reward. But don't worry, it won't happen."

Humor is everywhere and we all need to take advantage of it. If we don't laugh, we might cry, and we cry often enough.

 Write your own answers to these questions even if the thought can sometimes make you cry; there's a good chance that you can laugh about something here. It's a bit like writing your own "Redneck Jokes." You might feel guilty finding humor in this disorder—yes, it is serious—but if you take it too seriously and never find humor in it, you will lose your own mind.

Most unusual purchase or treasure?	
Longest "nap"?	
Most outrageous argument?	
Most grandiose claim?	
Most ridiculous rant?	
Most outlandish behavior?	
Strange thing you'd suggest to short circuit an episode.	
Favorite bipolar expression	
Translation of expression	

Button, Button, Who's got the Button?

Copy and clip these little buttons:

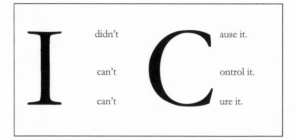

I ·

didn't

can't

can't

C

ause it.

ontrol it.

ure it.

WELCOME

…to an alternate reality

I Love You

In spite of yourself

Index

You can contact the author with questions, comments or just to chat. Questions and answers will be posted on the web site, so if there is something that was missed, check there or send in your questions.

Email: bonnie@getolife.org
AIM name –getolife
SecondLife name—Bonnie Godenot
Or through the web site at http://getolife.org

Purchase additional copies or other books by Bonnie Rice at http://getolife.org/mybooks or

Receive information on additional copies and other available materials by sending this coupon or the information requested to:
GET-O-LIFE Publishing
610 Payson Avenue
Quincy, IL 62301

Please send additional information packet for Love Has its Ups and Downs to

Name: _____

Address: _____

City: _____ State:_____

Zip Code: _____Phone: _____

Email Address: _____

☐ Send paper copies   ☐ Send by email

3247212R00068

Made in the USA
San Bernardino, CA
18 July 2013